Two Cities

Two Cities
New York and Brooklyn the Year The Great Bridge Opened

Margaret Latimer

Brooklyn Rediscovery
Brooklyn Educational & Cultural Alliance
Supported by grants from the **National Endowment for the Humanities**, a Federal agency, the New York State Legislature through a contract from the New York State Department of Education, the Consolidated Edison Company of New York, Inc., and other donors.

Brooklyn Educational & Cultural Alliance
Brooklyn Academy of Music
Brooklyn Botanic Garden
The Brooklyn Museum
Brooklyn Public Library
Long Island University—The Brooklyn Center
Polytechnic Institute of New York
Pratt Institute
St. Francis College
St. Joseph's College
The Long Island Historical Society (Associate)

Copyright © 1983 The Brooklyn Educational & Cultural Alliance
Library of Congress Catalog Card Number: 83-71020
ISBN 0-933250-09-06
Cover design: Jay Harris
Layout: Andrea Blumenfeld

Contents

Acknowledgments

The effort to recreate a year which occurred a century ago has involved the talents of many individuals and institutions. Their assistance and dedication have made the effort a most rewarding one.

Kenneth T. Jackson, David Ment, Bayrd Still, and Elliot Willensky reviewed early drafts and made valuable contributions. Sara Blackburn edited the manuscript. Among the many who provided information, documents, and visual materials were Phyllis Barr, Trinity Church; Reverend Calvin Butts, Abyssinian Baptist Church; Deborah Gardner, New York Stock Exchange; Reese V. Jenkins, Rutgers, the State University of New Jersey, Thomas A. Edison Papers; Stephen Levine; Peter Salwen; Steven W. Siegel, 92nd Street Young Men's & Young Women's Hebrew Association; John Tauranac, Metropolitan Transportation Authority; and Steven Wheeler, New York Stock Exchange. Steven Miller, Nancy Kessler-Post, and Jennifer Bright of the Museum of the City of New York turned a long-term search for contemporary visual materials into a pleasurable pursuit. Invaluable pictorial assistance was also provided by Elizabeth White and Peter Mehlin of the Brooklyn Public Library, and Marie Spina, former Brooklyn Public Library staff member; Patricia Flavin and Clare Lamers of the Long Island Historical Society, and Irving Menchik, who copied much of the visual material at the Society. Esther Brumberg took on a number of challenging problems of picture research. Other organizations which provided valuable information included: the American Jewish Historical Society; the Cathedral of St. John the Divine; the City College of the City University of New York, Archives; the libraries of Columbia University; Hunter College, Archives; the Library of Congress, particularly the Prints and Photographs, Manuscripts, and Geography and Map divisions; New York Bound; New York City Department of Health, Bureau of Vital Records; New York City Municipal Archives; New York City Municipal Reference Library; New-York Historical Society, Manuscript Division; New York Public Library, especially the Rare Book Division; New York University Archives and the Tamiment Library; Rensselaer Polytechnic Institute Library, Department of Special Collections; the Roman Catholic Diocese of New York; Rutgers University Library, Special Collections Department; and the Transport Workers Union.

David Ment provided background material on politics, water supply, and unions. Elizabeth Ferrer prepared background material on politics and provided considerable assistance throughout, and Rowan Murphy undertook painstaking research in numerous areas. Rebecca Helmers, Bernadette McCauley, Janice Spencer, and Elizabeth Wright were student interns during the project. The staffs of BECA, the BECA members, and Brooklyn Rediscovery were of continual assistance. For all the support and encouragement, I am very grateful. In the end, of course, final responsibility rests with the author.

Introduction

Much was written about the Great East River Bridge in 1883, the year it was completed. Little was written, however, about the two cities the Great Bridge joined. It was during the 1880s that America's final configuration was taking shape, and its urban fabric was emerging as a conspicuous quality of the nation's landscape. The bridge, which provided the first permanent link between the country's first and third largest cities, symbolized this process.

This study offers a brief glimpse of New York and Brooklyn as they were in 1883, a slice at one moment in time, a fleeting impression of daily life, of culture, poverty, wealth, politics, and society. It is written as though 1883 had recently ended, without the benefit of one hundred years of hindsight.

Because our study concerns one point in time—a single year that ends on December 31, 1883—much of what it contains has no ending, and only a few of the issues it describes are resolved. Just as in real life, very little ever comes to a finite termination. For the rest, then, the reader is invited to discover, on his or her own, the course of events that ensued after the last day of December in 1883.

View of New York and Brooklyn from New Jersey, printed on notepaper. (Museum of the City of New York)

New Year's, 1883

The year 1883 began much the same as previous years had begun. Just before midnight, thousands of the more spirited revelers from Manhattan, Brooklyn, and New Jersey packed into the streets by Trinity Church at Broadway and Wall to hear the ringing of the chimes and contribute their own cacophony of noises. The clamor was not confined merely to Wall Street, for throughout New York and Brooklyn there was scarcely any quiet to be found. At Trinity, however, much to the relief of the police and nearby residents, fewer people had turned out this year than last—but then this was a trend that had been noticed for quite a few years.

Before 12 . . . the firing of pistols, blowing of horns, & steam whistles, & the ringing of bells began, continuing for an hour or more and driving sleep from all eyes.

—Diary of Reverend
  John D. Wells

The next day, a fine, sunny, rather warm one for New Year's, the usual calls were made. In Brooklyn, the papers announced that Reverend Henry Ward Beecher of Plymouth Church would receive callers at his home at 124 Hicks Street, particularly those of modest means who had nowhere else to go. Some 1,000 stopped by. The Brooklyn financier and ferry owner, Henry E. Pierrepont, made calls on Mayor Seth Low, the Mayor's parents, the A.A. Lows, the John T. Martins, Mrs. Emily Roebling, the wife of the Chief Engineer of the Brooklyn Bridge, Congressman Henry Cruise Murphy's widow, and the industrialist A.T. White. Pierrepont noted in his diary that in most cases he merely left his calling card in the baskets hanging outside the doorways. His wife and daughter received about forty-five callers at their home on Pierrepont Place in Brooklyn Heights. In Brooklyn's Eastern District, Reverend John Dunlap Wells, pastor of the South Third Street Presbyterian Church of Williamsburgh, noted that there was less calling than usual; only fifty came to pay their respects, and a few others left cards.

In New York, Mrs. William H. Vanderbilt spent the morning at home on Fifth Avenue receiving callers, and in the afternoon Mr. Vanderbilt stepped out for a drive. And while Jay Gould was making calls, including one on Mrs. Vanderbilt, his wife was also receiving at their home. The papers noted that many fewer ladies of society were opening their homes to the practice that had been a tradition for so long, but again the decline had been occurring for some years.

While the traditions lingered from year to year, the two cities of New York and Brooklyn were growing with great speed. Both had expanded physically; in 1855 Brooklyn absorbed the city of Williamsburgh and the rest of the town of Bushwick to its north, and in 1874 New York had spread beyond its former boundaries of Manhattan Island, annexing that part of Westchester County west of the Bronx River and south of Yonkers. Both cities were expanding in population as well.

Manhattan's last remaining rural, farm, and unbuilt lands were disappearing rapidly. The elevated railways, which had been begun in 1878, reached the Harlem River by 1881, resulting in a considerable increase in the accessibility of the northern reaches of Manhattan from the business and commercial centers to the south. Although the leadership of Brooklyn was still contemplating the particulars of its elevated lines, the multitude of ferries, horse-car lines, stages, and steam railroads had spurred growth in that city.

Ever since 1820, when the U.S. Census had demonstrated New York's ascendancy over Philadelphia as the country's most populous city, New York had far outshone the rest of urbanizing America; after London and Paris, it was the third largest city in the world. The federal Census of 1880 indicated a total population for New York of about 1,200,000, nearly a thirty percent jump from 1870. Philadelphia stood second with 875,000, but Brooklyn came in for a close third with almost 600,000. For Brooklyn, this represented an increase of more than forty percent over the past decade.

The United States in 1880

The surge of New York City and Brooklyn was part of a larger national picture. The nation's population had reached a total of over fifty million by 1880, a jump of nearly one-third from 1870. Although the early decades of the nineteenth century had shown enormous expansion, there had been a marked decline in the growth rate during the 1860s with the intervention of the War of the Rebellion. Now, no one could deny that the country was growing fast. Its fifty million compared rather well to Germany's forty-five million and certainly overwhelmed Great Britain's fewer than thirty million.

As of 1880, America was comprised of thirty-eight states and several territories. In 1876, Colorado had become the thirty-eighth admitted to the one-hundred-year-old Union. In the early 1880s, the southern half of Dakota was agitating for statehood, and there was even talk of annexing Mexico and Canada.

Although the country was still predominately rural

—just over one-fourth of its citizens lived in cities—it was considerably more urban than just ten years previous, when not even one-fifth of the population was residing in cities. And while the overall population of the U.S. had increased by slightly over thirty percent between 1870 and 1880, the urban population had increased by over forty percent. Almost 4.25 million more people were living in America's cities in 1880 than had done so in 1870.

In 1880, New York and Brooklyn were two of twenty American cities with a population of over 100,000. Two decades earlier, they had been among just nine cities that had reached that size. New York, Philadelphia, and Brooklyn remained the top three, in the same positions they had occupied since 1860. And during the seventies, both Chicago and Boston had bypassed St. Louis, which in 1870 had been fourth in population.

The Census of 1880 reported that 6.5 million residents in America were black, and that almost an equal number were foreign-born. The country had begun to balk actively at the constant arrival of new populations, a great proportion of whom were processed through Castle Garden, the emigrant depot in the Battery at the southern tip of Manhattan. In 1882, the U.S. Congress had passed an act that severely restricted immigration from China.

Along with the burst in population, life was changing rapidly as well. The telegraph was making communication across the continent and the Atlantic a routine matter; the telephone, the elevator, and the electric light were adding new dimensions to urban life. Several railroad lines stretched across the country; the Northern Pacific Railroad was expected to be completed sometime in 1883. There was even talk about recent experiments with flying machines.

Every day seemed to bring major discoveries. A

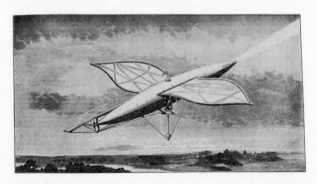

Professor Branowski's New Steam Flying Machine; successful experiments with a model in St. Petersburg were reported in the February 10, 1883 *Scientific American*. (Brooklyn Public Library)

German doctor, Robert Koch, had announced the identification of the tuberculosis bacillus, and a young Hungarian in Budapest, Nikola Tesla, recently had discovered the rotating magnetic field. The electric flat iron had been patented in 1882.

In the early eighties, world power was not so much shifting as it was slightly readjusting. Italy joined with Germany and Austria in forming the Triple Alliance in 1882. England was making strong moves in Egypt. Czar Alexander II had been assassinated in March 1881, replaced by his son, Alexander III. Several months later, United States President James A. Garfield was assassinated, and succeeded by Vice President Chester A. Arthur. The Italian patriot Giuseppe Garibaldi had died recently. Parnell was stirring up deep-rooted feelings for home rule in Ireland. And Stanley was still exploring the Congo.

Portrait of William H. Vanderbilt. (*Harper's Weekly*, March 18, 1882; Brooklyn Public Library)

Consolidation of big business was making a fairly new wealthy elite even wealthier. The Standard Oil Trust had formed, and its existence was just becoming public knowledge; the *Atlantic Monthly* had published a strong attack on the monopoly in its March 1881 issue. The *Chicago Daily News* of October 8, 1882 quoted William H. Vanderbilt as replying "the public be damned" in response to a reporter's question about complaints over cutbacks in service on his railroads.

In 1881, Clara Barton had established the American Association of the Red Cross in Washington, D.C. In Mississippi City, Mississippi, John L. Sullivan defeated Paddy Ryan as heavy-weight champion. Henry James had published *Portrait of a Lady* and *Washington Square* in 1881. Mark Twain seemed to be bringing out a book a year; his 1882 work was *The Prince and the Pauper.* New Englanders Ralph Waldo Emerson and Henry Wadsworth Longfellow had died in 1882, and their works were receiving renewed attention. Pierre August Renoir painted the *Luncheon of the Boating Party* in 1881. Europe and America were listening to the new works of Tchaikovsky, Saint-Säens, Brahms, Rimski-Korsakov, Offenbach, Wagner, and Gilbert and Sullivan. While some Americans were humming the "Barcarolle" from the *Tales of Hoffman,* others were singing "Good Night, Ladies."

The eastern United States suffered a terrible drought in 1881. Its intensity was felt all the more keenly in the urbanizing cities. In the West, there was virtually no more territory left to explore. The Indians were all but finally

11

conquered, and the reign of the legendary desperadoes was coming to an end. The Earp brothers did receive some attention in October as the result of quite a lot of shooting at the O.K. Corral outside Tombstone in Arizona Territory. Sometime later, the retired Jesse James was shot in the back of the head by one of his own men at St. Joseph, Missouri. And telegraph services had relayed in fine detail that William H. Bonney—alias Billy the Kid—had been caught by Sheriff Pat Garrett and shot dead in New Mexico Territory. What passed almost unnoticed was that this last symbol of the lawless West had been born in a tenement on New York City's lower east side some twenty-one years earlier.

Back East, New Yorkers and their brethren across the East River were finding time to complain about all the ills of urban living: the potholes, the traffic, the high cost of transportation, the lack of police protection, the filthy streets and dreadful sewer odors, the shortage of water, the overcrowding of classrooms, the ever-present corruption in politics, the proliferation of overhead telegraph, telephone, and electric wires, and the great difficulty of finding a decent place to live for a reasonable price. In spite of such perennial problems, New York and Brooklyn were booming. Both cities were building rapidly, and new means of accessibility were being added or extended every year.

The Two Cities Enter the Eighties

The ubiquitous pothole portrayed here on Brooklyn's Bedford Avenue. (The Long Island Historical Society)

New York clearly was the country's center of finance and economic power. Gould, Astor, Vanderbilt, Villard,

The Brush electric arc light in Madison Square. (*Harper's Weekly*, January 14, 1882; Brooklyn Public Library)

Napoleon Sarony's portrait of Lilly Langtry at the time of her debut appearance in New York. (Library of Congress)

and Morgan were among its most prominent business figures. The Astors and Vanderbilts rivaled each other over how much they could bring under their respective dominions. Jay Gould, already in command of the city's elevated railways, took control of the Western Union Telegraph Company in 1881. Henry Villard took over the Northern Pacific Railroad the same year. J.P. Morgan owned one of the largest banks in the world.

With the extension of rapid transit, no area of Manhattan was unreachable. The apartment had become an acceptable mode of living for the well-to-do. An elegant apartment building was going up on 72nd Street, just west of Central Park. It had been dubbed "The Dakota," presumably by skeptics who considered the territory west of the park to be just that remote.

The parks of the two cities—namely Central and Prospect—were the subjects of constant admiration. In 1881, an Egyptian obelisk, affectionately called "Cleopatra's Needle," had been erected in Central Park, but not without angry accusations that the park was being desecrated. The brand new boulevards leading from Brooklyn's Prospect Park—Eastern and Ocean Parkways—were considered among the finest drives in the region.

Electric lighting was beginning to transform the appearance of New York City and would soon be introduced into Brooklyn. Gigantic poles 160 feet tall—as high as some church steeples—had been installed by the Brush Electric Illuminating Company in Madison and Union Squares. Brush arc lights were also illuminating stretches of Broadway, Fifth Avenue, and several of the side streets in the shopping district. On September 4, 1882, the Edison Electric Illuminating Company turned on its generators at 257 Pearl Street in lower Manhattan, providing electricity for its first fifty-nine commercial customers—including J.P. Morgan's bank, the *New York Herald,* and *The New York Times*.

The cities were endowed with a vast array of splendid cultural attractions that offered the latest acclaimed talent, much of it imported from Europe. In January of '82, Oscar Wilde had created a sensation with his first American lecture, held at Chickering Hall on Fifth Avenue. In April, P. T. Barnum's enormous purchase from the London Zoo—Jumbo the elephant—debuted at Madison Square Garden as part of Barnum & Bailey's Circus. And when the captivating "Jersey Lily," Lillie Langtry, made her American debut at Wallack's Theatre in November, the drama critics were rebuked for treating her as harshly as they might any other actress.

As usual, big city politics were in constant turmoil. Boss Tweed had died in jail back in 1878, but few were so naive to think that his Tammany organization had died with him. Death had also taken former Tammany mayor Fernando Wood in 1881, and former Brooklyn mayor and U.S. Congressman Henry Cruise Murphy in late 1882. In January 1883, New York inaugurated its new governor, Grover Cleveland, and New York City its new mayor, Franklin Edson.

At the beginning of '83, France's gift to America, Frédéric Auguste Bartholdi's massive statue of *Liberty Enlightening the World,* had appeared close to being actually installed on Bedloe's Island in New York harbor. Plans had been afoot for so long that no one quite seemed to remember its original purpose: to commemorate the end of American slavery, to observe the centennial of American independence, or simply to acknowledge the friendship between the two nations. In spite of the display of Liberty's enormous arm at the 1876 centennial exposition in Philadelphia, and later in Madison Square, contributions for the statue's base, which had to be paid for by America, were coming in very slowly. But it seemed that 1883 might finally be the year that the first bridge across the East River would open. After more than thirteen years of construction, even the most patient observers had begun to wonder whether the cities of Brooklyn and New York would ever really be connected. For many, the statue and the bridge signified the promise of the city.

Brooklyn photographer George Brainerd captured the new Brooklyn Bridge rising up over his city. (Brooklyn Public Library, Brooklyn Collection)

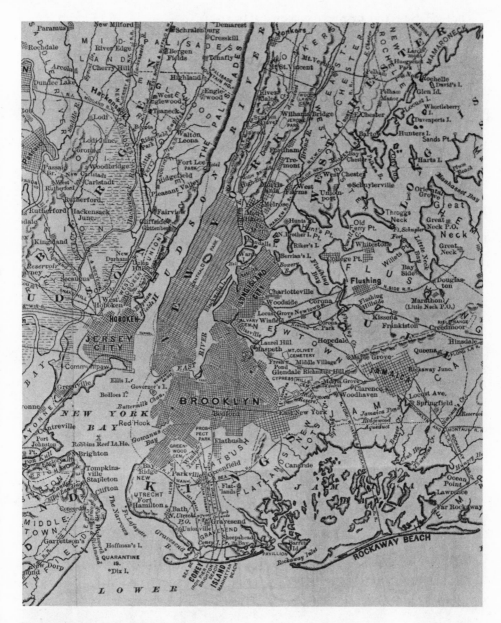

Map showing New York and Brooklyn. (*Appleton's Dictionary of New York and Its Vicinity*, 1884; Willensky Collection)

The Shape of the Cities

In 1883, New York City was composed of two parts: the island of Manhattan and the Annexed District, the land that had been part of Westchester until 1874. Manhattan stretched about thirteen and one-half miles from the Battery north to the Harlem River and measured a little more than two and one-quarter miles across at its widest point. The half-way point was at about 80th Street. Across the Harlem River, the Annexed District added only another two and one-half miles to the city's length. But because the new area was considerably wider than Manhattan, the annexation nearly doubled the city's previous 14,000 acres.

The City of Brooklyn, occupying the northern third of the much larger county of Kings, was somewhat under 14,000 acres in area. Almost square in shape, it was not quite seven miles in length and five miles at its widest. Comprising roughly that portion of the county from Newtown Creek on the north down through Prospect Park on the south, the City of Brooklyn included the formerly separate communities of Brooklyn, Williamsburgh, Greenpoint, and Bushwick.

The two cities were complete entities unto themselves. Some forty years earlier, however, while New York was a bustling hub of over 300,000, the new City of Brooklyn could barely boast one-tenth of that. In spite of its size in 1880, and the fact that it contained all the elements necessary to be labeled a city, Brooklyn was still considered a bedroom for New York.

The major governmental, business, commercial, and

Brooklyn: Everything in Its Place

View from the Brooklyn tower of the new bridge, looking southeast toward downtown Brooklyn . (The Long Island Historical Society)

George Brainerd's photograph of the heart of Brooklyn's commercial district, looking north from City Hall Square. (Brooklyn Public Library, Brooklyn Collection)

In many respects . . . [Brooklyn] is like New York. It has its political rings, its academies of music and design, and it has many other things that New York boasts of—all, however, pitched in a minor key.

—*Appletons' Dictionary of New York*

This general store on Neck Road in Gravesend also served as the local post office. (The Long Island Historical Society)

cultural quarters of the city were arrayed around the City Hall, which was at Fulton and Court Streets, three-quarters of a mile up the hill from the Fulton Ferry, the most frequented mode of transportation to Manhattan. Within a radius of half a mile of City Hall could be found the new Municipal Building, the Kings County Court House, the Academy of Music, half a dozen theaters, the Music Hall, the Brooklyn Library, the Atheneum, the Art Association, and the Long Island Historical Society. The main retail shops, the banks, and the business offices were lined along Fulton and adjacent streets.

To the north of downtown was the Navy Yard, and immediately beyond that, Williamsburgh, Greenpoint, and Bushwick, all of which was now called Brooklyn's "Eastern District." Williamsburgh, known locally as "the burgh," contained an active commercial center of its own. The dome of its most imposing building, the Williamsburgh Savings Bank on Broadway, could be seen from great distances. And although industry stretched all along Brooklyn's East River waterfront, it was primarily concentrated here in the Eastern District.

To the south and east of City Hall lay Brooklyn's major residential areas. Prospect Park, about two miles from City Hall, had been planned in the 1860s to be located near where the people were going to live, a projection that was proving its accuracy in the 1880s.

The vast remainder of Kings County, comprised of the towns of Flatbush, New Utrecht, Gravesend, Flatlands, and New Lots, included fewer than 33,000 residents. The towns consisted largely of small, quiet communities—with the exception of New Lots, which, with its bustling settlement of East New York, accounted for 14,000 inhabitants. Gravesend was more typical. The town, which stretched down to include Sheepshead Bay and Coney Island, had a population of fewer than 3,700. New Utrecht, with fewer than 5,000, contained several rural villages, such as Bath, on Gravesend Bay, and the pleasant summer resort of Bay Ridge, on the Narrows. Flatbush, a lovely suburban town of almost 8,000, many of them old Dutch families, was known for its gracious tree-lined lanes as well as for its fussiness about who lived within its borders. Canarsie, a village in Flatlands on Jamaica Bay, was referred to in the guidebooks as being a resort of modest hotels and known for its excellent fish and clams.

Self-contained, physically independent, and politically autonomous, Brooklyn was nevertheless always being compared with New York. The very fact of its proximity to the city responsible for so much of its growth generated a special irony: Brooklyn was a city that never stopped struggling for its own identity.

It had taken two and a half centuries for New York to move uptown. Until the 1880s, almost all building had taken place below 59th Street. But by 1883, almost 19,000 structures had been completed above that point. Now the dense settlement of all of Manhattan could be envisioned. Printing House Square, the area that had been at the northern end of town when New York's City Hall was completed in 1812, was now in what had become lower Manhattan, at the New York terminus of the new Brook-

Conolly's Store on the waterfront in Bay Ridge. (The Long Island Historical Society)

New York: Change on Top of Change

By the 1880s, New York had grown far north of City Hall; Printing House Square and the new Brooklyn Bridge are to the right. (Museum of the City of New York)

lyn Bridge. To the north were the slums and working-class neighborhoods that were relegated to a diversity of immigrant groups, and a congested mix of miscellaneous industrial and commercial activity. As the city's population thrust northward, so did New York's commercial and cultural center continually move uptown. In the 1880s, it was pausing along Broadway and Sixth Avenue, between Union Square at 14th Street and Madison Square at 23rd Street.

Fifth Avenue was still the address of old New York society, but it was gradually being overtaken by commercial spillover from the shopping district. The areas to the east of Madison and west of Sixth were already tenement districts and specialized commercial centers inhabited by

The commercialization of Fifth Avenue, here at the northwest corner of Madison Square at 26th Street, with the Hotel Brunswick. (Museum of the City of New York)

small businesses. And as the elevateds pushed farther uptown, so did the residential areas, with the city's central spine remaining more elegant than the flanking avenues.

By the 1880s, with the convenience of the existing New York and Harlem Railroad, as well as a number of horse-car lines and the newly completed elevated railways, substantial portions of the east side had been developed. The settled areas reached up past Murray Hill in the east 30s and Grand Central Depot at 42nd Street to Yorkville in the 80s and Harlem at 125th Street. To the west were the still quiet communities of Bloomingdale west of Central Park, Manhattanville in the 120s, Carmansville at 150th, and Washington Heights and Inwood at the northern end of the island. The old Bloomingdale Road, the extension of Broadway which ran from 59th

Bird's-eye view of Central Park looking north, with 59th Street in the foreground and the still rural west side on the left. (Benson Lossing, *History of New York City*, 1884; The Long Island Historical Society)

Street north, had been realigned and rebuilt into a handsome thoroughfare—the Boulevard—and in 1880, overlooking the Hudson River north of 72nd Street, a parkway, Riverside Drive, had opened.

The Annexed District, the former towns of Morrisania, West Farms, and Kingsbridge, which formed New York City's 23rd and 24th Wards, was beginning to show signs of growth, albeit small ones. Morrisania in particular had been attracting population, accessible as it was by the New York and Harlem from Grand Central, and by the els which connected with horse-car lines over the Harlem River. Most of the old estates had been sold off, and the former town was clearly taking on a suburban character; it was composed largely of small cottages and modest homes, many available for rent rather than sale. And Riverdale, overlooking the Hudson, contained a number of fine suburban villas that housed prominent New York businessmen. The community prided itself on not having a single store.

During 1883, the Suburban Rapid Transit Company began building a bridge to carry rapid transit across the Harlem River. A second company, the New York, Fordham, and Bronx Railway, was organized at the end of '83 for the purpose of constructing elevated railways in the District. And while much of New York was expanding, certain things never seemed to change. As far as anyone could tell, the financial district, centered on Wall Street, was always going to be exactly where it was.

Construction activity at Kingsbridge Road and Webster Avenue in New York's Annexed District. (Museum of the City of New York)

Commerce and Industry

For some decades New York City had been emerging visibly as the commercial and financial hub of the country. While finance and wholesale and retail trade continued to center in Manhattan, some of the flourishing industrial sector began to look to Brooklyn as an ideal location for new development.

"The Street"

In 1880, Wall Street—or "the Street"—was the heart of financial activity in New York, and thus, of the nation. The major banking houses, the Stock Exchange, the Custom House, and the Sub-treasury were located either on the Street or only a short walk away.

It was estimated that behind its white marble walls, the New York Stock Exchange on Broad, just south of Wall, handled some nine or ten billion dollars in transactions in one year. Wall Street skeptics warned that investing in Wall Street had become rather risky. One writer estimated that on a daily basis only about 10,000 of 300,000 shares traded were for "legitimate investment."[1] The rest were traded on speculation. The "curbstone brokers" outside on Broad Street were considered to be even less reliable than those within the Exchange.

The Produce Exchange, a massive brick and terracotta structure designed by George B. Post, was going up just north of Battery Park on the east side of Bowling Green. The papers marveled over its size, with its 220- by 144-foot main hall projected to be the largest trading floor in the world. Its tower was sure to be a major landmark. The New York Cotton Exchange, also designed by Post, was getting a new building at Beaver and William.

Of the banks and insurance companies, probably J.P. Morgan's Drexel, Morgan & Company at Wall and Broad predominated over all the others, but First National, City National, Chemical National, and Chase National banks were all nearby. And Kuhn & Loeb, the large investment banking firm said to be close in rivaling Drexel, Morgan, was located on Nassau just north of Wall. Some of the savings institutions were also in the financial district, but others, such as the Bowery, Dry Dock, Greenwich, and Harlem Savings banks, were in more residential neighborhoods. Many, founded as associations for the working classes, remained in the same neighborhoods where they had begun. The Bowery Savings Bank, for example, was still where it had been since 1834, at 130 Bowery just

Lithograph of Wall Street looking toward the New York Stock Exchange on Broad; Drexel, Morgan & Company is on the left. (Museum of the City of New York)

21

north of Grand Street. Brooklyn housed many branches of the New York banks; it also had a number of its own, particularly savings banks, such as the Brooklyn Savings Bank, the Williamsburgh Savings Bank, and the Dime Savings Bank. Both cities had a full roster of fire, life, and marine insurance companies as well.

Two facilities of the federal government also were situated on the Street. The former Merchants' Exchange, with its stately row of ionic columns on the south side of Wall between William and Hanover, contained the U.S. Custom House, the center of foreign trade in the city. And on the north side of Wall, opposite Drexel, Morgan, stood the U.S. Sub-treasury, whose vaults held an immense sum of currency.

Like everything else in the two cities, the financial institutions were expanding. The Manhattan Company and the Merchants' National banks were building on Wall Street between Broadway and Nassau, and in Brooklyn, the Dime was about to erect a new two-story stone-front building at Court and Remsen Streets.

To meet the demands stimulated by the enormous increase in financial activity since the recovery from the Panic of 1873, a new type of structure was rising: the office building, in which space could be rented by individual companies according to their particular needs. The Mills Building on Broad opposite the Stock Exchange was having great success, and Brooklynite Henry E. Pierrepont was campaigning hard to convince his Board of Directors of Green-Wood Cemetery, which maintained an office in Manhattan, to rent one of the upper floors in Cyrus Field's new thirteen-story Washington Building, on the west side of Bowling Green opposite the Produce Exchange. Pierrepont's directors were rather wary of relying upon an elevator, and advised him to look elsewhere.

One of the occupants of the Mills Building was Henry Villard, who had moved there from offices in what had once been a mansion at Fifth Avenue and 9th Street. With the idea of completing a railroad to the Northwest, he had persuaded a number of prominent financiers to invest in the Northern Pacific Railroad. In spite of rumors on the Street that the railroad's success hinged largely on attracting a sufficient population to settle along its route, Villard was pushing for a grand opening ceremony in the fall.

The latest innovation in scaffolding, allowing through access for pedestrians, at the Manhattan Company and Merchants' National Bank construction site on Wall Street. (*Scientific American*, December 15, 1883; Brooklyn Public Library)

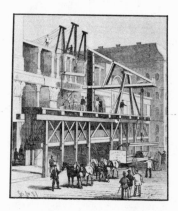

Wall and Broad looking west toward the enduring Trinity Church at Broadway. (Museum of the City of New York)

View of the tip of Manhattan, looking northeast; the vessels are moored around the Castle Garden emigrant depot at the Battery; both the Produce Exchange on the right and the Washington Building at the center are still under construction; to the left is the spire of Trinity Church. (New-York Historical Society)

Wall Street will preserve its character as long as the cosmetropolis endures. Banking, exchange, stocks, insurance . . . speculation, and financial and commercial agencies from all parts of the world will circle around Trinity Church until its walls crumble.

—W.C. Conant

The Industrial Fabric

Amidst all the flurry of activity stood the solitary and solemn Trinity Church. Its site on Broadway at the end of Wall had been occupied by a succession of Trinity Churches; the present building, by architect James Renwick, had been there since 1846. Trinity gave the Street a semblance of calm and stability. With its spire, it had long been the tallest structure in the country. Now the towers of the Brooklyn Bridge were rivaling it.

According to the 1880 Census of Manufacturing, New York City had some 11,000 factories employing over 200,000 people, and Brooklyn had some 5,000 factories employing 49,000. New York contained substantially more industrial capital than Brooklyn, but because of the crowding of Manhattan's industrial districts, and with less and less space available for landing, loading, and storage, New York's manufacturers were beginning to look elsewhere to build.

View from the Produce Exchange northeast toward the Brooklyn Bridge; the light building in the center is the Cotton Exchange. (Museum of the City of New York)

23

Much of Manhattan's manufacturing took place in the lower portions of the island. Heavy industry, such as iron foundries, was located along the waterfront, while the manufacturing of consumer items, such as textiles and clothing, was located inland. The leather center was called "the Swamp," a designation that referred to the formerly swampy district behind Printing House Square just south of the new Brooklyn Bridge and running east to about Pearl Street. The middle west side of New York also housed substantial industry. The Higgins Carpet Factory on West 44th Street covered more than a city block and employed around 2,000 workers. The carriage industry was located around 45th and Broadway, giving rise to the name "Longacre Square," after the carriage district of London. The biggest firm was Brewster & Co. on Broadway between 47th and 48th, with its warerooms at Fifth Avenue and 42nd Street.

Most of Brooklyn's industry stretched up and down the East River from Newtown Creek down through Greenpoint and Williamsburgh, around the Navy Yard and downtown, to Red Hook in South Brooklyn, and along the Gowanus Bay and Canal. Greenpoint and Williamsburgh were the centers for metal foundries, glass, porcelain, and pottery works, oil refineries, breweries, printing plants, glue factories, and heavy machinery manufactories. The companies, such as Poulson & Eger, iron founders on North 11th Street in Williamsburgh, often had their offices in Manhattan—in this case, on West 23rd Street. The Astral Oil Works of Charles Pratt, part of Standard Oil, stood at the northern edge of Williamsburgh. The Union Porcelain Works, producing some of the country's finest decorative china, was expanding its facilities near Greenpoint Avenue. D. Appleton & Company had its mammoth printing and binding plant just east of the Brooklyn Navy Yard. Royal Baking Powder and Charles Pfizer & Company, chemicals, were nearby. From Atlantic Avenue at the southern edge of downtown to Red Hook, could be found a diversity of manufacturers. The Ansonia Clock Company had recently built a large factory at 12th Street, up the hill from the Gowanus.

With such a large population, the region was an obvious center for food processing. One of the biggest food operations was the beef slaughterhouse. Although the advent of the refrigerated railroad car was making it possible to ship the carcass directly from Chicago, much of the

Advertisement for Royal Baking Powder, manufactured in Brooklyn. (*Harper's Weekly*, January 27, 1883; Brooklyn Public Library)

work still took place at the destination point. Most of New York's slaughterhouses were concentrated on the East River in the low 40s and along the Hudson between 40th and 57th. Since 1876 there had been some regulation of slaughterhouses below 110th Street, but the intolerable conditions they created were far from alleviated. The cattle were driven through the streets, putrid odors emanated from discarded decaying matter and rendering plants, and offal was dumped directly into the harbor, adding up to a situation the Board of Health seemed unable to rectify.

Sugar, coffee, and flour were just a few of the bulky produce items handled in Brooklyn. Massive grain elevators, some five or six stories high, lined much of Brooklyn's waterfront, handling about three-quarters of all grain that came into the port of New York. Brooklyn's largest firm, the Havemeyer & Elder sugar refinery, had suffered a devastating fire in 1881. It was now rebuilding on its waterfront site in Williamsburgh what would be the largest facility of its kind in the world, destined to produce an estimated 1.2 million pounds of sugar each day.

Brooklyn was also manufacturing the products required to preserve food. Refrigerators were just coming into use, particularly in commercial establishments, and improved methods were being introduced to keep the ice from melting too rapidly. One of the biggest suppliers of ice, the Knickerbocker Ice Company, had depots all up and down the two cities' shores.

Much of the food for both cities ended up in Manhattan's wholesale district. The area, which was largely below Canal Street, centering around Chambers and West Broadway, was filled with the cast-iron-fronted commercial buildings that had been so popular since before the War. One of the largest wholesale grocers, H.K. and F.B. Thurber & Co., was at 116 Reade Street. The retailers generally picked up their own goods from the wholesalers. Grocers were beginning to establish chains. Thomas Anderson, a dealer in teas, had over a dozen outlets. A considerable amount of produce was sold through the city's markets. The major ones, Washington on the lower west side, Fulton just south of the new Brooklyn Bridge, and Jefferson in Greenwich Village, were all in the process of getting new buildings in 1883. In addition to the permanent markets, numerous informal ones sprouted up all over. A farmers' market was situated along the Hudson at Gansevoort Street in Greenwich Village, and every Saturday evening a low-priced open-air produce market was held on the Bowery around Grand. Another and even poorer food market appeared on Saturday nights at 42nd Street west of Eighth Avenue.

The Port

Since their earliest days, the cities' waterfronts were crucial to their prosperity. The shores of each were lined with wharves, warehouses, ship yards, sundry manufacturers, lumber and coal yards, ferry slips, and passenger and freight steamship piers. The entire port handled about two-thirds of the foreign commerce entering the country, and accommodated the arrival and departure of about 20,000 ships each year. But there was some concern developing that New Jersey was beginning to take business away from the New York and Brooklyn waterfronts.

Manhattan's waterfront commerce was crowded together on the southern portion of the island. On the East River between South Ferry at the island's southern end, and Grand Street, only one and one-quarter miles north, one could find large sailing vessels, some canal boats carrying grain, a number of ferries, the fish market, and several dry docks, iron foundries, and lumber yards. The Hudson shore, however, was becoming much more active than that along the East River, whose space had long been used up. From the Battery to 23rd Street, in addition to numerous ferries, was an agglomeration of the piers of the major passenger and freight shipping companies: the trans-Atlantic steamship lines, the domestic and foreign freight lines, and the Fall River, Boston, Hudson River, and excursion steamboat lines.

While New York's waterfront commerce was concentrated in Manhattan's toe, Brooklyn's maritime and waterfront industries lined almost all of its East River shore. And while New York handled much of the port's dry goods, Brooklyn was occupied with a large share of heavier goods. Piers for ocean-going ships attracted the patronage of ten cargo and passenger steamship lines. In addition to the oil refineries, foundries, sugar refineries, grain elevators, and warehouses that spread along the Brooklyn waterfront, there were also a number of modern maritime facilities, such as the Atlantic and Erie basins in South Brooklyn. The Atlantic Basin's docks, it was said, could handle 150 sizable vessels at one time.

South Street along the busy East River waterfront. (Museum of the City of New York)

The Retail Trade

By the 1870s, New York had become the retail market for the country. In recent years a new concept in retailing had developed: the concentration of a variety of merchandise in large dry-goods establishments. The clothing manufacturing and wholesale center remained downtown, around Broadway south of Houston, while the retail center and the large dry-goods stores moved steadily northward with the population. Nevertheless, the old retail center at Grand Street remained very busy, featuring lower-priced stores that attracted the less affluent. Lord & Taylor's old dome-topped store on Grand now catered to the less expensive taste. Ridley & Sons, also on Grand Street, attracted bargain-seekers from both Manhattan's east side and Brooklyn's Eastern District.

The busy Grand Street retail center, looking east from the Second Avenue elevated. (Museum of the City of New York)

The finer stores were located farther uptown, around Broadway and Sixth Avenue between Union and Madison Squares. R.H. Macy & Company at Sixth Avenue near Union Square had prices somewhat higher than those at Ridley's. By '83 it offered more than thirty departments, and a ladies' lunchroom which it claimed to be the first in the country. The more fashionable of the large stores were slightly to the north of Union Square. In 1872, Lord & Taylor had opened one of the early iron-clad retail structures in New York at Broadway and 20th. Nearby were B. Altman & Company and the new store of Arnold, Constable & Company. Way uptown on its own was Bloomingdale Brothers, at Third Avenue and 55th Street, which drew residents of moderate means.

. . . went around to L & Taylors and got 4 pairs of drawers & 6 shirts & 6 collars.

—Reginald Fairfax Harrison, age 14

27

Manhattan's retail center had an abundance of specialty shops which catered to every taste. Some of the more exclusive were situated around Union Square: Tiffany & Company, fine imported goods; F.A.O. Schwarz, toys; the Gorham Manufacturing Company, silversmiths; Brentano Brothers, books; and G. Schirmer, importers and publishers of music. To the south, not far from Washington Square, were two other dealers in silver, Reed & Barton and Rogers Brothers, and the book dealer, Charles Scribner's Sons. Brooks Brothers, the men's specialty store, was also there, but word had it that it was about to build another shop on Broadway in the 20s.

Up Sixth Avenue across from Arnold, Constable was W. & J. Sloane, which specialized in carpets; Gorham was building a new store there as well. A little farther north

Trade card for Cammeyer's shoe store at Sixth Avenue and 12th Street, "one block from Macy's." (Museum of the City of New York)

was Knoedler & Company, at Fifth Avenue and 22nd, which contained a branch of Goupil's, a Paris gallery, and G.P. Putnam's Sons, the book store, was on 23rd. Best & Company's Liliputian Bazaar, which claimed to be the only outfitter of children's clothes, had recently moved to West 23rd near Sixth Avenue. A popular spot for eyeglasses was Meyrowitz Brothers, just off East 23rd.

Where Manhattan's retail emporiums were scattered, Brooklyn's were mostly concentrated downtown, along a short stretch of Fulton Street. Wechsler & Abraham at Fulton and Tillary was a pleasant, all-purpose store. Its spring 1883 sale, with "Talismanic Prices," featured silk dress goods, misses' double-breasted cloaks, Damask napkins, Nottingham lace curtains, and Oriental rugs.[2] Baldwin's, claiming to be the largest retail men's clothing store in the two cities, had its Brooklyn store on Fulton and a huge Manhattan outlet at Broadway and Canal. It promoted business through its monthly publication, employing such mottos as "the best advertising medium is a pleased customer."[3] Ovington's, on Fulton and Clinton, was Brooklyn's most select specialty store, offering the finest in imported glass, chinaware, and ornamental pieces. After a fire in January, it constructed a new brick and terra-cotta building on the same site. The new store boasted crystal chandeliers as well as the novel curiosity, steam heat.

Best & Company's first delivery wagon at its first run in 1883. (Museum of the City of New York)

The fashionable stores of New York and Brooklyn had both spring and fall openings, and a number of them put out two catalogues each year for mail-order customers. The end of a season was marked by clearance sales. The stores, which generally had little ventilation, usually closed on Saturday afternoons in the heat of summer. Christmas was the biggest season; in 1883, Macy's began to install steam-powered moving toys as part of its Christmas window display.

Manhattan was filled with minor shopping districts. Both Third and Eighth Avenues—Third up to the 130s in Harlem and Eighth up to the 40s—were lined with small, generally cheap, retail stores. Pawnbrokers and low-cost bric-a-brac shops were centered around Chatham Street, the Bowery, and Third Avenue up to about 4th Street. Second-hand furniture stores were scattered along Seventh and Eighth Avenues. Street peddlers crowded many of the shopping streets, and in the early eighties, there were over

It is the duty of the police to arrest all unlicensed keepers whose stands project beyond the stoop lines, but they do not do it.

—Harry H. Marks on
  street peddlers

800 municipally-licensed peddler stands; the one-dollar licenses were obtainable through the local alderman.

A large work force, including a sizable proportion of women and immigrants, was employed in the business and industry of the two cities. Nearly 725,000 men, women, and children worked in a wide variety of professional, skilled, and unskilled occupations. The standard work week for employees was six days, with hours in Wall Street offices as well as retail shops extending from about 7:30 a.m. to 6:00 p.m. By the 1880s, hours were beginning to loosen slightly. Some workers were given Saturday afternoons off in July and August, and a privileged few were beginning to be let off every Saturday afternoon. The work day was also shrinking, to hours that began at 8:00 or 8:30 in the morning and ended at 5:00 or 5:30. Legal holidays were rare, but some firms were beginning to give one- and sometimes two-week vacations with pay in the summer. Factory workers had longer work days, from around 6:30 or 7:00 a.m. to 6:00 p.m. Laborers had far stricter lunch breaks, and they were allowed far less time off than their office and shop counterparts enjoyed.

Nearly 200,000 women in New York and Brooklyn depended upon their wages for their livelihoods. A number had distinguished themselves in a wide variety of professions, such as charity, medicine, journalism, and fashion. Middle-class women might be employed as department heads in large dry-goods stores, or as teachers, even principals, in the public schools. Those of more modest means worked as shop girls, domestic servants, governesses, or cooks. Almost no women were employed on Wall Street; although the typewriter was in common use, almost all secretaries were men.

By far the largest number of women workers were employed in factories. Of these, most worked in textiles and clothing, glass and china, bookbinding, and cigar making. In 1883, some 2,000 women and girls were employed in bookbinding, which was considered a desirable occupation. A considerable number of women in the cigar and garment industries worked in their own homes or in tenement factories under miserable conditions.

The early 1880s was a time of confrontation between employer and worker, as the industrialization of the country grew and ownership began to be concentrated more

The Workers

Workers at the paper-wetting machine at the *New York World*. (*Scientific American*, March 4, 1882; Brooklyn Public Library)

Naturally the work is very unhealthy. . . . Large quantities of the fine dust of the tobacco is inhaled, frequently causing lung diseases and the poisonous vapor exuded by the damp leaf renders the atmosphere of the workshops perfectly stifling.

—Harry H. Marks on the cigar factory

Cigar Makers' International Union leader Samuel Gompers. (New York Public Library Picture Collection)

and more in the hands of fewer and fewer. A variety of unions had been formed to counter the power of the industrial corporations, and there was a movement to increase labor's strength by amalgamating the unions on a regional and national basis. The Noble and Holy Order of the Knights of Labor was the fastest growing national organization with a membership of nearly 52,000 in 1883. More influential were the local councils of trade unions, of which New York City's Central Labor Union (CLU) was the most active and famous. Comprised, in 1883, of more than twenty unions with a combined membership of nearly 10,000, the CLU was socialistic in spirit; it pioneered in political as well as economic action. At its meeting on December 30, 1883, the CLU declared a boycott of the *New York Tribune* as well as the newspaper's advertisers, in support of a strike by Typographical Union Local 6.

In February 1883, the Cigar Makers' International Union (CIU), led by Samuel Gompers, managed to convince the State Legislature to outlaw the manufacture of cigars in New York tenements. The union was effectively aided by Assemblyman Theodore Roosevelt, who, after observing the shocking labor conditions at first hand, worked toward the bill's passage and then helped assure its signing by Governor Cleveland. According to the CIU's *Cigar Makers' Official Journal*, the law would bring about the "abolition of Sunday and all-night work," which would provide jobs for "at least 3,000 who are now idle and almost starving."[4]

During most of 1883, the cigar workers were preoccupied by a factional conflict. Under Gompers and his associates, the CIU was working toward a strong

Advertisement for chewing tobacco, manufactured in New York. (*Trow's New York City Directory*, 1883-4)

organization with good union benefits. A socialist faction, made up principally of Central European immigrants and primarily concerned about the larger workers' movement, seceded in 1882 and formed the Cigar Makers' Progressive Union. After about 400 workers, mostly Progressives, walked out of the East 23rd Street factory of S. Ottenberg & Brothers in July, a number of the Internationals abandoned the walkout and returned to work. Ottenberg, however, succeeded in getting the support of the manufacturers' association, resulting in the lockout of some 8,000 workers, members of both unions. The Progressives held a mass meeting at Irving Hall on 15th Street just east of Union Square, while the Internationals let the employers take care of defeating the Progressives through the lockout. When the lockout ended in early August, the hostility between the two groups was far more intense than before.

The telegraph industry was also hit with a major labor action in 1883. Fully established as a dominant national corporation, and having been taken over in 1881 by Jay Gould, the Western Union Telegraph Company gradually obtained almost total power to control the wages and work conditions of telegraph workers throughout the country. By 1883, only one year after achieving formal status as an affiliate of the Knights of Labor, the Brotherhood of Telegraphers had built a membership of more than 10,000 primarily skilled workers.

In the spring, the union moved to present Western Union with a full set of demands: an eight-hour day, a substantial wage increase, equal pay for men and women. After a complete standoff, the union struck on July 19th. The action halted a great deal of the telegraphic communication throughout the country, substantially affecting the normal conduct of business. Traders on the New York Produce Exchange adopted a resolution sympathizing with the union's grievances and offering to raise funds to aid the strikers. *The New York Times* considered that the "cavalier treatment" by Western Union had "succeeded in throwing the sympathy of the public wholly on the side of the striking operators."[5] Gould, maintaining the upper hand all the while, managed to keep partial operations going by closing down some branches and hiring almost anyone he could as a strikebreaker. Although the strikers had saved a little money on their own, and the Knights of Labor raised donations through appeals and contributed

Mr. Voytisek . . . the leading spirit in the Progressive Union . . . called . . . attention . . . to the fact that this was the first instance in the history of American labor movements in which employers combined together to lock out their workmen and to crush them because they demanded their rights as citizens.

—*The New York Times* on the Irving Hall meeting

The monotonous clicking of the telegraph instruments in the main operating room . . . was abruptly broken in upon at 12:11 o'clock yesterday afternoon, by a prolonged screech from a small pocket whistle, blown by one of the operators. . . . This was the prearranged signal for the beginning of the movement ordered by the Telegraphers Brotherhood.

—*The New York Times*

some out of its own general fund, there was hardly enough to enable the workers to stay out for long. By mid-August, the strike was called off. While Western Union estimated it had lost about $700,000, Jay Gould knew that it had been worth every cent.

If the employers held vast power in some industries, workers had some strength—at least temporarily—in others. Because of the requirements of the business, those who labored in the construction industry had considerable say. The work of carpenters, bricklayers, plasterers, painters, and iron workers had to be timed carefully and coordinated with all stages of construction. The workers understood that with a union shop, they could maintain a substantial degree of control. In early August, rushing to complete the Metropolitan Opera House in time for its scheduled opening in the fall, its architect, J.C. Cady, snubbed a group of representatives of the Allied Building Trades Union who had come to determine the number of union and non-union workmen on the project. Within a few moments, 250 men were on strike. The next morning, the representatives were back, the non-union workers were persuaded to join the union, and work resumed. One week later, union delegates found fifty non-union plasterers at work on the Dakota Apartments and nearby row houses. They refused to join the union, whereupon all the union workers left the site. By the next morning, the non-union plasterers had changed their minds, and the bricklayers, plumbers, and gas fitters returned. Charging that this was the "tyranny of the trades unions in its most offensive form," the *Times* looked to a period when the building boom declined and employers would once again "have the whip hand."[6]

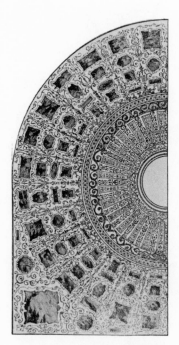

Detail of the intricate ceiling design for the new Metropolitan Opera House. (*Harper's New Monthly Magazine*, November 1883; Brooklyn Public Library)

Neighborhoods and Housing

As New York and Brooklyn expanded in population and land area, the nature of their settlements changed enormously. What had been small, compact enclaves clearly differentiated from the estates and farmland beyond, became a series of diverse communities, one running into the next and filling up much of the territory within the cities' borders.

Brooklyn's residential neighborhoods were clustered around its central downtown. The most elite was the Heights, to the west of City Hall overlooking the harbor. It had been a popular suburb for Wall Street for over half a century. By 1880, the Heights was almost entirely filled with stately brick and brownstone row houses, with a sprinkling of elegant detached mansions. To the south, on the other side of Atlantic Avenue and the ferry connecting Manhattan with the Long Island Railroad, lay a row house community nearly as distinctive as the Heights. The areas just to the north and farther to the south were comprised primarily of modest row housing and flats occupied largely by the working classes and immigrant groups. "The Patch," a squatters' area centered around Fourth Avenue and Butler Street, was considered the worst district in the city. To the south of the Gowanus and west of Green-Wood Cemetery, a solid working-class neighborhood was developing, with many of the tenants employed on the waterfront.

To the east of downtown lay "the Hill." Its streets were lined with fine brownstones, and at its peak stood the mansions of a number of Brooklyn's industrial elite. Farther east of "the Hill," in Bedford, and to the southwest, on the west side of Prospect Park, new streets were filling up with rows of fine town houses, although both areas possessed a number of free-standing mansions as well. To the north of the Navy Yard, Williamsburgh and the remainder of the Eastern District were fairly built up with solid working- and middle-class housing. Greenpoint was a community of small, neat row houses, and along Bushwick Avenue, a number of the local industrialists— brewers, for the most part—had built their sumptuous homes.

At the beginning of 1883, of New York City's estimated 100,000 buildings, about three-fourths were predominantly residential. Of the nearly 3,000 buildings added during the year, most were erected for dwelling purposes.

Cook Street in the built-up portion of Bushwick. (The Long Island Historical Society)

Estimates ran that between twenty and twenty-five thousand of the city's residential buildings were tenements, generally referring to a building with three or more families. These were said to house a total of anywhere from 500,000 to 900,000 people. Guidebooks pointed out that two types of tenement dwellers existed: the relatively well-off working people, who could have afforded better housing if they chose to live anywhere but in New York, and the very poor. And there were two types of tenements: those specifically constructed as tenements, and older, single-family houses which had been adapted to multi-family use when their original owners moved uptown or to Brooklyn. Critics deplored the entire array, whether they were narrow three-story houses divided up into six or more units, or wider five- or six-story buildings that held twenty or more families.

The whole of residential lower Manhattan was now given over to tenement housing of one sort or another, and the larger tenement buildings were rising all the time. As Manhattan extended northward, the tenements followed, occupying large swaths in the very eastern and western portions of the city, flanking the industry along the rivers on one side and the middle-class neighborhoods on the other. The 4th Ward just above and below the new Brooklyn Bridge had the reputation of being one of the most unfortunate sections of the city. The area known as

Five Points, on the western edge of the 4th Ward around the junction of Worth, Mulberry, Baxter, and Park Streets, although not quite as notorious as when Charles Dickens recounted its horrors in the 1840s, was still synonymous with decay and misery. Corlear's Hook, the point where the island jutted out into the East River at Grand Street, had a similar reputation. A step lower than the tenement was the shanty, many examples of which could be found clustered around the upper ends of Central Park, near the slaughterhouses along the East River, and scattered about the unbuilt portions of the east and west sides.

Persuasive testimony about and personal observation of the dreadful conditions endemic to tenement housing— dangerous and unsanitary situations, the threat of fire, and the lack of light and air—spurred the State to pass special tenement house legislation pertaining to New York City and Brooklyn in 1867 and 1879, but neither law had much effect. A city's Board of Health was left considerable leeway in interpreting the rather vague standards, or it could simply hire too few staff to receive complaints and carry out enforcement proceedings. On top of this, the builders, believing they did not gain sufficient profit from constructing tenements, endeavored to cut as many corners as they could.

James E. Ware's prize-winning tenement design, submitted to the 1879 competition of the journal *Plumbing and Sanitary Engineer,* was attracting more builders to the tenement field, particularly by demonstrating how the buildings could be constructed economically in long rows. Those engineers dedicated to sanitary reform praised the Ware plan beause it allowed for shafts along each building's sides to provide openings for light and air; it also recommended the allotment of two water closets per floor. Some critics observed that the proposed shafts would be magnets for refuse and subsequent fires, and that they would result in excessive stench, noise, and too little ventilation and light.

A.T. White of Brooklyn, believing that any form of tenement bred evil, began to build model housing for workers and their families. His Tower and Home Buildings on Hicks Street in South Brooklyn, completed between 1877 and 1879, were constructed around large yards, and each flat contained some plumbing and more than a minimal amount of light and ventilation. Proclaiming that philanthropy and profit were not impossible companions, White wanted to illustrate that building decent housing for workers could also be a good business proposition. Drawing upon his example, the Improved Dwell-

Tenements don't pay as they used to, and . . . only a certain class of people care to own property of this kind. Poor people make bad tenants.

—Interview with tenement resident

36

Rendering of A.T. White's housing for workers in South Brooklyn. (The Long Island Historical Society)

ings Association was founded in 1879 to provide decent living space for workers. The association completed one model project in Manhattan, on First Avenue in the low 70s. And Trinity Church had built some housing for workers along with a factory and warehouses in the area bounded by Hudson, Greenwich, Charlton, and Vandam Streets in Greenwich Village.

In spite of these efforts, the squalid tenement still predominated. The architects worried about the dangerous building heights and the lack of structural controls. The sanitary engineers fretted over the lack of decent plumbing conditions. A typhus scare underscored the serious health problems; in May, six cases were reported in one tenement alone, on West 117th Street. But an attempt in the State Legislature to pass a new and tougher tenement house law was abandoned by the spring of 1883.

Just as they lingered over the presence of the tenement house, the authors of guidebooks loved to categorize Manhattan's 12,000 boardinghouses. South of 8th Street were the cheaper boardinghouses for clerks and salespeople, often attached to cheap restaurants known as "hashhouses." Above 8th Street were the better houses. The north-south avenues also offered points of demarcation, with the houses along Fifth Avenue being the most expensive, and the rents dropping as one moved east or west.

Having overcome their earlier prejudices, by the early 1880s quite a few middle- and upper-middle-class New Yorkers had forsaken the row house and were living in apartments, and in the even newer "cooperatives." A

I'm established in one of the most comfortable of those boardinghouses that constitute a vast camp flanking Fifth Avenue, and which range from the serving-girl's sleeping closet in Eighth Street to the palatial quarters, with prices to match that prevail near Central Park.

—Short story heroine's letter home

number of apartment buildings had been constructed in the late 1870s, particularly for fashionable young and not-so-young bachelors, who found such lodgings suited their purposes ideally. The better-class apartments were those around Madison Square. Adequate accommodations could be found around Union Square, but below Washington Square, flats were considered cheap and patronized largely by foreigners. The Studio Building was established on West 10th Street as working or living quarters for artists. John La Farge, William Merritt Chase, and Frederic Church were among the tenants in '83.

Apartments for couples and families were beginning to become popular. For some years, there was great concern that the middle class had fled Manhattan because of the exorbitant cost of housing. Hopes were high that with the new accessibility to all areas of the island, those who had left for Brooklyn and New Jersey might return to the city. The area of greatest demand for apartments was below 59th Street, and the prices were high. The "French flat," a fancy name for an apartment, could demand an equally fancy price.

The cooperative, or "home club," was beginning to attract some attention. Its participants reasoned that, ostensibly, a more modestly priced apartment could be had if all the tenants formed an association, sharing the costs among themelves rather than paying rent plus overhead to a third party. But costs were rising, and the co-ops were proving to be expensive to build and maintain. Some rather posh projects were under way: the Dakota, the Berkshire on East 53rd, and the Gramercy on Gramercy Park. The most elaborate complex—being called the "Spanish Flats"—was going up on the south side of Central Park between Sixth and Seventh Avenues. Each of its buildings—which the developer, a Mr. Navarro, designated with such romantic names as the "Barcelona," "Madrid," "Granada," and the like—would contain a large central court and be organized as its own club.

For the wealthier classes, the single-family residence —whether part of a row or free-standing—was still the preferred form of housing. The row house was the more predominant. Between three and four stories tall with a basement, it was generally twenty-five feet wide. The ground floor was divided into a dining room in front and a kitchen, with a laundry or servant's room in back. More recently, the front room was being called the "billiard

Madison Avenue, looking south from 70th Street. (Museum of the City of New York)

room." The first floor, entered from the stoop, contained a front and back parlor, with the back parlor now often used as the dining room, and a butler's pantry in back, joined to the kitchen below by a dumb-waiter. The upper stories were devoted to sleeping, with a front and rear chamber separated by closets and dressing rooms, each with a wash basin. The top floor might have a number of smaller rooms for servants, and often contained a sink and a storage tank for water.

All newly built better housing contained interior plumbing, and older houses were being fitted with a variety of facilities. The toilet (the water closet or "W.C."), the wash basin—often with both hot and cold running water—and the bathtub came in various materials and designs. These fixtures were generally encased in wooden cabinets to cover up what were often ugly appearances and faulty installation. Although the State Legislature passed some plumbing regulations, the sanitary engineers still warned of inadequate plumbing methods, and the risks of faulty venting systems. By the end of '83, the new law was appearing to have achieved some good results, but problems tended to be alleviated only when a major misfortune occurred.

One other type of housing was common in the cities: the hotel. Just as with almost everything else, there existed a careful social and economic ordering of hotels.

A great many people . . . pass much more time than is necessary in the unusually unwholesome atmosphere of [the W.C.], taking books and newspapers with them. This is a vicious habit which entails more than one evil consequence upon those who practice it. . . .

—James C. Bayles, *House Drainage and Water Service*

39

Those that lay below 42nd Street catered to transients, and those situated above it housed permanent residents. Traveling businessmen and merchants from out of town frequented the Broadway hotels below 14th, such as the Grand Central, near West 3rd, the Metropolitan, below Houston, and the venerable Astor House, opposite the Post Office. A number of popular, reasonably-priced hotels were located around Union Square. There were many low-priced hotels at the southern end of Manhattan, particularly on the lower west side, which lodged workers in the wholesale districts and recent arrivals from Castle Garden. The cheapest hotels stretched along the Bowery.

Many of the better hotels were situated around Madison Square. The Fifth Avenue Hotel, probably New York's best known, had long been Republican state headquarters, and all the Presidents stayed there on their visits to the city. The Hoffman House drew sporting men and politicians as well. Across the way, the Albermarle was very quiet in comparison, catering to refined visitors from abroad. It had gained some notoriety, however, with the recent visits of the actresses Sarah Bernhardt and Mrs. Langtry. The Brunswick appealed to a variety of guests that ranged from English tourists and railroad men to those who were simply drawn to its fine restaurant.

Farther uptown, the Grand Union Hotel, across 42nd Street from Grand Central Depot, served the transient. A new hotel, to be called the Murray Hill, was going up a block away. The Windsor on Fifth Avenue in the mid-40s, it was said, drew permanent residents who stayed for the winter and went to the country for the summer. It also served as a transient hotel for prominent merchants and magnates, particularly those in railroads. The new rich from Fifth and Madison, such as Gould and Vanderbilt, were often seen in conference with associates in the small parlor off the 46th street entrance.

Brooklyn's hotels were known to be very solid and not too fancy. Mansion House on Hicks Street was the best known, and others included the Pierrepont House on Montague, Clinton House on Fulton near the retail stores, and the Franklin House and the Fulton House, by the ferry.

Future Directions

There was no question that both cities were experiencing a building boom. In Brooklyn, over 1,000 persons were employed in the building trades. There were some forty architects, four hundred builders, and three hundred real estate agents. Many of the some 2,400 buildings constructed in 1883 were going up on speculation. The demand for quality housing, nowhere close to being met, was particularly great in the area around Prospect Park. Bedford was about half developed, and were it not for its poor accessibility, it would have been much further along. The western half of Greenpoint by the East River was pretty well filled up, but not much activity was going on in the rather swampy eastern half. Builders were busy constructing low-cost housing in South Brooklyn.

The *Brooklyn Eagle* saw only promise for a city "practically unrivalled in this part of the country."[7] The opening of the new bridge was sure to influence prices and rents. But some felt that the building of an elevated would be even more of a decisive force in the city's growth.

Across the river in New York, so much building was taking place that it was almost impossible to detect the trends. New building was now less a result of real estate speculation than of real demand. In past years, the New

Preparation for the construction of row houses in Bedford, on what had been the McDonough farm. (The Long Island Historical Society)

41

A photograph by Peter Babb looking north from George Ehret's roof at Fourth Avenue and 94th Street; the railroad tracks from Grand Central Depot are seen emerging from the tunnel to cross a viaduct through Harlem. (Museum of the City of New York)

York and Harlem Railroad had helped to spur development in the direction of Harlem. With new modes of access in more recent years, there were moves in other directions as well. With the Ninth Avenue elevated completed, for example, the relatively underdeveloped west side would probably be filled up within a decade. The lower portion of Manhattan between Washington Square and 59th Street was still the most desirable, and costly apartments, many with elevators, were being built on every available lot. The intrusion of commercial activity on lower Fifth Avenue was giving rise to speculation that the new Riverside Drive, or Eighth Avenue, flanking Central Park—or even Washington Heights, at the northern end of the island—could become the future home of New York's aristocracy. And once the elevated railways were extended across the Harlem River, one could predict a burst of development in the Annexed District.

If the encroachments of trade increase in the next 10 years as they have done during the past 10, Fifth-avenue . . . will be given up almost entirely to business and wealthy men will be forced to . . . build their residences in the side streets or far enough up town to be for a while longer beyond the reach of the growing trade. . . .

—*The New York Times*

A view of the Harlem River between Manhattan and the Annexed District, as it would look in about 1885. (*Harper's Weekly,* November 18, 1882; Brooklyn Public Library)

A photograph taken from a construction site on the newly developing west side looking south at 72nd Street and the intersection of the Boulevard and Tenth Avenue. (Museum of the City of New York)

Some speculators foresaw a time when the recent phenomenon of the steam-powered elevator would make it possible for two million residents to be accommodated in Manhattan alone. And some even believed that there might be a day when the island could hold five million and not appear crowded at all.

Building by Design

The Brooklyn Bridge, the foundations of which are built of limestone, may rot in a few generations.

—*American Architecture and Building News*

The tall red brick house in Thirty-fourth Street, by [McKim, Mead & White], which looks less like a work of architectural art than a magnified piece of furniture "with the Chippendale feeling," can scarcely be called successful.

—Critique of the "new departure" style

Nearly three-quarters of New York's buildings were clad in brick or stone, and the rest in wood, with only a tiny portion in cast iron. In contrast, over half of Brooklyn's were wood sheathed. The architectural and building journals often predicted the imminent decay of the cities' structures. As a result of climatic conditions and the poor quality of building materials, the brownstones and marble-fronted buildings were experiencing serious deterioration.

The architecture of the two cities provoked every epithet imaginable: monotonous, chaotic, frivolous, bland, monumental, insignificant, garish, affected, or unintelligible. Whenever a building's style was an indecipherable amalgam of diverse elements, it would be labeled "Queen Anne." There was great hope that the two cities would soon see an end of the dreary brownstone and hideous cast-iron-fronted edifices that had been so popular in recent decades.

The Pauper and the Millionaire

In 1883, as far as the press was concerned New York was suffering from a peculiar paradox. On the one hand, decent housing was so costly that only old society and the very well-to-do could afford to live there. On the other, the city was saturated with tenement districts and wretched slums, making it an involuntary haven for the poor and the immigrant as well.

Because of this vexing contradiction, the press dismissed those who were not perceptibly wealthy as members of the poorer classes, as though there existed nothing in between. In the same fashion, the communities in which these "poorer classes" lived were generally referred to as slums. The slums, in turn, were labeled according to the ethnic identity that prevailed most widely in

Year after year New York seems to justify the painful, dispiriting averment that it is a city of paupers and millionaires.

—*Harper's New Monthly Magazine*

An illustrator's portrayal of the life of the poor. (*Harper's Weekly*, July 28, 1882; Brooklyn Public Library)

each. Thus, immigrants and minority groups were inextricably associated with the slum.

During the previous decade, the number of immigrants and racial minorities had increased significantly. Immigrants now made up forty percent of New York's population and about thirty percent of Brooklyn's. In 1883, nearly 400,000 came through Castle Garden from other lands.

Ethnic Complexity

By 1880, New York City's black population numbered nearly 20,000, an increase of fifty percent over 1870. The black residents of New York had been confined largely to what the press called "Little Africa," an area south of Washington Square centering around Thompson and Sullivan Streets. By the late 1870s, new immigrant groups had begun to move into this sector, forcing the blacks out. The dislocated were moving primarily to the far west side, around the west 20s and further north. Many of Brooklyn's almost 10,000 blacks had moved there from Manhattan in the early 1860s and were now living in the Fort Greene area of "the Hill," and some were beginning to move further east into Bedford and East New York. Excluded from many occupations, most blacks were employed as domestics or laborers, although the European immigrant was beginning to displace the black in the domestic field.

From 1,000 to 2,000 Chinese lived in a very poor tenement area on the lower parts of Baxter and Mott Streets. A small number also lived in Williamsburgh, in the Eastern District. Of all the immigrant populations, the Chinese were probably the most abused by the press. Ignoring the great majority of upright, hardworking Chinese, the journalists liked to associate them with opium dens, which they continually deplored as sinister temptations to the innocent middle class.

"Little Germany" stood east of Second Avenue between Houston and East 14th Streets. The Bowery, the neighborhood's active shopping street, had become even

A strolling photographer in Chinatown, drawn by A.B. Shults. (*Harper's Weekly*, August 25, 1882; Brooklyn Public Library)

45

more hectic with four horse-car tracks on its surface and the elevated line overhead. East of First Avenue between Bleecker and 12th Streets was a concentration of some 15,000 Bohemians, largely in the cigar-making, tailoring, and shoemaking trades; they were often cited in the weeklies as socialist agitators. Groups of prosperous Germans still lived further downtown, off East Broadway, as well as uptown in Yorkville. A sizable number of middle- and upper-middle class Germans lived in the Bushwick and Williamsburgh sections of Brooklyn. In all, the two cities contained some 200,000 Germans.

About one-fifth of New York's population, and about one-tenth of Brooklyn's, was of Irish birth. The journals would have one believe that all Irishmen were politicians, policemen, or saloon keepers. The old 4th Ward and the far east side in the 20s were the primary Irish tenement areas. In Brooklyn, the more prosperous Irish lived just south of the Heights, while the working-class lived close to the industrial areas of South Brooklyn and the East River waterfront.

New York's some 10,000 Italians were located around Five Points, Baxter and Crosby Streets, and Wooster and Sullivan Streets south of Washington Square, in addition to a newer settlement that was growing west of the Bowery along Mulberry and Mott Streets. Only about 1,000 lived in Brooklyn. The press categorized the Italians as day laborers, rag pickers, and organ grinders, but

"Exiles from Russia—Their First Day in New York." (*Harper's Weekly*, February 18, 1882; Brooklyn Public Library)

admitted that some had achieved a higher status and worked as waiters, musicians, or language teachers.

Most of the eighty to ninety thousand Jews in the two cities lived uptown, or in Brooklyn's Bedford section; the great majority was of German background, with a smaller number of Sephardic Jews, but almost all were middle- or upper-class. While the existence of poor Jews was not a new phenomenon, their dramatic increase was. With the mounting persecution of Jews under the new Czar, more and more Russian Jews were emigrating to America, many trying to find their way in New York. Because they were not welcome elsewhere, the great majority were settling in an existing community of poor Jews around Hester, Chrystie, and Eldridge Streets, or in Williamsburgh in Brooklyn. The local tenement landlords were known to charge them particularly high rents—because, they claimed, if they rented to Jews, they could rent to no one else.

The Affluent

Detail of George B. Post's design for one of the Fifth Avenue Vanderbilt mansions, this one on 57th Street. (*Harper's New Monthly Magazine*, September 1883; Brooklyn Public Library)

The well-to-do of New York and Brooklyn, just as the poor, followed discernable settlement patterns. In Manhattan, the wealthy were moving uptown, but not all were moving in the same way. The "old set," for the most part, remained steadfast on lower Fifth and Madison Avenues around the squares. William Rhinelander Stewart, the philanthropist and a commissioner of the State Board of Charities, lived just north of Madison Square, and his mother, Mrs. Lispenard Stewart and the Edward Coopers (he was Peter's son and former Mayor of New York), resided at Washington Square North. The ninety-two-year-old Peter Cooper, manufacturer, inventor, and founder of the Cooper Union, lived with his son-in-law, Congressman Abram Hewitt, at the corner of Lexington and 22nd.

Some of the children of the old set had moved uptown. Assemblyman Theodore Roosevelt, for example, resided on West 45th Street. The "middle set," those in well-established industries such as oil and railroads, were moving up from Murray Hill (in the 30s) to Fifth and Madison near the new St. Patrick's. The Vanderbilts seemed to be taking over the west side of Fifth Avenue in the 50s. Richard Morris Hunt designed a chateau for William K. Vanderbilt, son of William H., on the northwest corner of Fifth and 52nd. William H. had an ornate double house built for himself and two daughters on the next block down. And up at 57th Street, George B. Post was building another palace for yet another of William H.'s sons. Jay Gould also lived on Fifth, just north of the Windsor Hotel.

Henry Villard of the Northern Pacific Railway expected to be moving during the year from Fifth Avenue between 33rd and 34th, where a number of the Astors lived, to Madison Avenue between 50th and 51st directly behind St. Patrick's. He asked Stanford White of McKim, Mead & White to design an Italian-style palace, actually a grouping of houses, the largest of which he would occupy. J.P. Morgan was staying put at his brownstone mansion in Murray Hill on Madison and East 37th. August Belmont, Jr., lived two blocks away, on East 35th. Rumors had it that A.T. Stewart's grand marble-clad mansion on Fifth Avenue nearby was being put up for rent to a commercial tenant, which quite worried the neighborhood. Some of the newer, or newest, money was taking the plunge across 59th Street. McKim, Mead & White was planning an ornate mansion at 72nd and Madison for Charles L. Tiffany, who was now living in Murray Hill. And the homes of brewers Jacob Ruppert and George Ehret were up farther, in the underdeveloped east 90s, not far from their Yorkville breweries.

Engraving of shipping merchant A.A. Low, father of Brooklyn's mayor. (The Long Island Historical Society)

The wealthy families of Brooklyn tended to live in the Heights. The stately brownstones of merchants A.A. Low, A.M. White, and Henry E. Pierrepont overlooked the harbor on Pierrepont Place, while the houses of their progeny generally were located somewhat more modestly inland. Although the Heights was comprised largely of row housing, a number of sizable mansions were sprinkled

Art gallery in John T. Martin's house on Pierrepont Street in the Heights. (The Long Island Historical Society)

48

about, such as the commanding home of clothing manufacturer John T. Martin. Some of the newer money lived on "the Hill"—the Pratts of Astral Oil on Clinton Avenue, for example, and the Pfizers on Washington Avenue.

Domestic Life

The contrast between the daily life of the rich and poor was, of course, immense. For the tenement dweller, only the bare necessities were possible; for the affluent, clutter was "in." The more bric-a-brac from Tiffany's or the top floor of Ovington's, the more Oriental rugs from W.& J. Sloane, and the more paintings from Goupil's, the better.

Increasingly elaborate gas heating systems were available for better homes and apartments. The newly formed New York Steam Company was offering to supply steam power and heat to consumers through underground pipes. Because steam was considered efficient but very hard to regulate, most homes still used gas.

The tenement generally was lighted by kerosene lamps or candles, the apartment and house by gas. A few of the very wealthy, too far from Edison's power plant, were having their own generators installed to produce the

The new bridge, a popular image in advertising, was employed here to help promote the sewing machine. (Library of Congress)

new electric lighting. J.P. Morgan had Edison install electricity in his Murray Hill home. In spite of the fact that the generator didn't work all that well and that he was constantly nagged by neighbors complaining about its noise and vibrations, his Drexel, Morgan, became one of Edison's earliest customers, and Morgan himself became a large investor in the Edison company.

The tenement flat usually contained a cast-iron, wood-burning stove; the more well-to-do might have purchased a gas range, which was being heavily promoted by the local gas companies. The tenement dweller relied on a stove for cooking as well as heating water and the flat iron, while the better-off probably had hot and cold running water as well as a gas iron. The public was still a little dubious about gas appliances. The ice box, or refrigerator, was beginning to be found in better homes, although brewers and restaurants were still the largest consumers of ice.

Demonstration of a gas stove at the annual fair of the American Institute. (*Scientific American*, October 29, 1881; Brooklyn Public Library)

"Best Meat, Fruit, and Ice Preserver in the world," claimed refrigerator manufacturer Alex M. Lesley, Broadway and 35th, Manhattan. (*Lain's Brooklyn Directory for the Year Ending May 1st, 1884.*)

Food of enormous variety was available for purchase, as long as one could afford it. Consumers feared the possible contamination of many items: meat, fruit, vegetables, milk, and, of course, water. The boiling of water and milk was recommended to remove impurities, and housewives were advised to add citric or hydrochloric

Announcement of a newly patented can opener. (*Scientific American*, July 28, 1883; Brooklyn Public Library)

Nana "knew her place" and did not mind sleeping in a little cold room on the fourth floor with the other servants. . . .

—Nathalie Smith Dana

Dining Out

Chops mean to most Americans a bone scraped quite white, with a small piece of scalloped paper at one end, and a morsel of thin, tasteless meat at the other.

—*Appletons' Dictionary of New York*

acid before boiling water to disguise the unpleasant taste found once it was boiled.

Beef prices had been going down as a result of the easier shipping permitted by refrigerated cars. Heavy rains in late June of 1883 seriously damaged the New York and Connecticut strawberry and cherry crops. In late July the Fulton and other markets were featuring watermelons from the Carolinas and Georgia, sold cheaply by the slice. Vegetables were plentiful and inexpensive and included beets, cabbage, carrots, cucumbers, egg-plant, tomatoes, peas, lima beans, summer squash, red and green peppers, red cabbage, string beans, watercress, parsley, chicory, Irish and sweet potatoes, and turnips. Frozen salmon was available, but soft-shell crabs, just beginning to arrive, were still costly.

Staples were relatively high priced. White flour was considerably more expensive than plain. White sugar would be seen at the table, but brown was used in the kitchen. Oleomargarine, butterine, and other butter substitutes were available but distrusted, and one could never even be sure that the butter sold was really pure butter. Canned food was becoming more common.

Grocers on occasion provided delivery to the house, but more often, a genteel family would dispatch a member of the household staff to do the shopping. The prosperous might have two or more in domestic help, perhaps a chambermaid or chambermaid-waitress, or a laundress-cook, a butler or butler-second man, or a coachman or coachman-groom. The papers contained numerous advertisements daily, all stressing the desired characteristics for a proper household employee: "respectable," "protestant," and "references." Families were warned, however, that many who advertised were not what they seemed, and that the "intelligence offices" found on most business streets were a much more reliable source for domestics.

Without a doubt, New York's finest restaurant was Delmonico's, at Fifth Avenue and 26th, and almost every major function seems to have taken place there. The Hotel Brunswick and Hoffman House were also known to have particularly excellent kitchens. The chop-house was nearly unknown in the U.S., although a fair lamb chop could be had at both the Astor House and the Parker House (at Broadway and 34th). Each was known to serve ladies. Gentlewomen frequented Clark's on West 23rd, and Purs-

Trade card for a Harlem restaurant specializing in Viennese cuisine. (Museum of the City of New York)

sell's and the Vienna Bakery on Broadway. Jacques on West 11th, the Hotel Hungaria on Union Square, and Moretti's, one block west, served international cuisine. A good, modestly priced lunch could be found at the German lunchrooms of Koster & Bial's on Park Place, and at the Rathskeller in the basement of the Staats-Zeitung building in Printing House Square. There was known to be an excellent French restaurant on the Bronx River, way up in the Annexed District, and the newly built McGowan's Pass Tavern had opened in '83 at the north end of Central Park, over the loud protests of those who looked at it as just another park intrusion.

Inexpensive restaurants were plentiful, from the fifteen-cent hash-house to the oyster bar. Saloons ranged from the most elegant, like the one at Hoffman House, to the darkest hovel near Five Points. A free lunch was offered at the respectable Irish pub, where, for the price of a beer, one could help oneself to a fairly hearty repast.

If one were to inquire as to what was the most popular food in New York, he or she would undoubtedly discover that it was the oyster, and that it was in evidence both at Delmonico's and at the dankest oyster saloon. One oyster fanatic, in fact, proposed adding an ''r'' to the months of May, June, July, and August just so the delectable morsels could be eaten the year round.

Porcelain oyster plate made at the Union Porcelain Works, Greenpoint. (The Brooklyn Museum, gift of H. Randolph Lever Fund)

Governing the Cities

Since the War of the Rebellion, the acceptance of the expanding role of government had grown markedly. Local government had taken over from private or volunteer organizations the responsibilities of police and fire protection and had assumed greater control of street paving and repair, lighting, water supply, and sanitation. At the same time that the cities took on additional or expanded powers, their administrators protested that their limited budgets could not possibly permit the delivery of adequate services.

The Delivery of Services

New York's and Brooklyn's local governments were organized along similar lines. Each had a Mayor, a Board of Aldermen, departments of Finance, Public Works (City Works, in Brooklyn), Excise, Docks, Law, Public Parks, Police, Fire, Health, and Public Charities and Corrections, and each its own Board of Education. In Brooklyn, jurisdiction over functions such as charities and corrections was divided between the City and Kings County.

Law enforcement was of major concern to the residents of both cities. New York's Police Department, whose headquarters was on Mulberry Street in lower Manhattan, had some thirty-four station houses and a force of 3,000. Brooklyn had seventeen station houses with about 1,150 men. The demand for an increased force was heard constantly in both cities.

The fire departments of the two cities had moved a long way from the days when they were strictly volunteer and largely associated with one or another political faction. New York's department boasted 51 engine companies and 17 hook-and-ladder companies, and more than 709 fire alarm boxes, connected to the central office by telegraph wires. Sliding poles had just been introduced in the fire houses and were considered immensely helpful in getting firemen to the scene. Many buildings now had fire escapes. Yet all of this did not stop disastrous fires such as the January 1882 conflagration at the old World Building at Park Row and Beekman Street, in which most of the dozen who died perished because the ladders could not reach them. And in early February 1883, the lack of adequate safety precautions resulted in the death of over a dozen children and injuries to many more at the school of the Most Holy Redeemer on East 4th Street between Avenues A and B.

Brooklyn's total of twenty engine companies and

New York City Mayor, Franklin Edson. (New York Public Library Picture Collection)

five hook-and-ladder companies was considered extremely paltry next to the facilties and equipment of almost any other major city. Several disastrous fires in 1883 proved that even with the new sliding poles, more fire alarm boxes and hydrants, and an agreement with New York to borrow its equipment in emergencies, a serious situation existed.

The two cities' parks departments seemed to fare much better, although neither escaped the usual grumblings about the condition of the parks. Manhattan's favorite was Central Park. Except for the shanty-dwellers who lived along its boundaries, the park was left almost entirely to the pleasures of those well-to-do who owned a carriage, could afford the transit, or lived in the neighborhood. The Park Commissioners were often criticized for straying from the original plans of its designers, Frederick Law Olmsted and Calvert Vaux, and in general, for neglecting the park. In 1883, the abandoned Arsenal, a "repulsive-looking barrack" now "given over to bats and owls" was the bone of contention. The ponds and lakes with "their thick and slimy ooze" were considered so unsanitary that unless money were appropriated immediately for their restoration, it seemed imperative that they be drained and filled.[8]

Brooklyn enjoyed many open spaces, including Washington Park (or Fort Greene), City Park near the Navy Yard, Carroll Park in South Brooklyn, Tompkins Square in Bedford, and, of course, the glorious Prospect Park. Conceived by the same designers as Central Park, Prospect was heavily used—by an estimated five million in '83—and the constant demand for more facilities, such as tennis courts, worried Brooklyn's Park Commissioners. Although barely a decade had passed since Prospect's completion, the Commissioners ordered the removal of a large amount of what they considered to be overgrown greenery, an action that was attacked with great passion. The Commissioners also infuriated the public by announcing that now that they were to take final possession of the Litchfield family mansion, which was on park property, they were thinking of using it as Parks headquarters. Responding to immediate suggestions that a museum might prove to be more appropriate, the Commissioners insisted that such a facility would cost too much, and that, besides, the Long Island Historical Society and the Art Association served in that capacity quite well.

Great care was taken to observe the plan adopted in the original scheme of planting . . . and while much desirable material was necessarily destroyed, it was with decided advantage to the general results.

—Park Commission Report
on Prospect Park

The departments of public works oversaw many of the cities' basic functions. Brooklyn's Commissioner, Ripley Ropes, for example, presided over a Chief Engineer (whose jurisdiction included street lighting and public baths), a Water Purveyor, a Registrar of Water Rates, and superintendents of Sewers, Streets, and Supplies.

At the beginning of 1883, Brooklyn had only three public baths—outdoor pools that were situated at the river's edge. These were used by 260,000 men, women, and children each year, a great number of whom had no bathing facilities where they lived. The city promised four new baths by the end of the year. New York's nine public baths, all located at the lower end of the island along the two rivers, served nearly 4,000 daily between June and October. They were open four days a week for males and two for females.

The provision of street lamps was another public works function. Brooklyn, not yet wired for electric lighting, had some 15,000 gas lamps in '83, serviced by eight

Women's day at a New York public bath. (*Harper's Weekly,* September 2, 1882; Brooklyn Public Library)

separate gas companies. New York had 24,000 gas lamps, and by the end of '83 there were 128 electric arc lights in its streets and parks.

New Yorkers considered their city the worst paved in the world. It was estimated that 357 miles of Manhattan's streets were paved in some form, with materials that included Belgian block and cobblestone as well as the new, experimental macadam. Nearly seven miles of streets were mapped and paved for the first time in '83, most of them in the low and middle 100s. Some streets considerably to the south of these were also paved, including Beekman Place between East 49th and 51st Streets. Even with all the street repaving, Manhattan's heavy increase in horse-drawn traffic of all sorts, the severe winters, and the constant digging up for the laying of pipes and wires were resulting in extraordinary wear and tear.

A far smaller proportion of Brooklyn's streets was paved, but its street problems were far less serious than New York's. The papers noted, for example, that the well-used Eastern and Ocean Parkways needed repair, but that resurfacing with gravel would do the job.

Public Works was also responsible for street cleaning. In New York, private contractors cleaned the streets south of 14th, and the department was responsible for those above, with the debris eventually emptied into scows, towed by steam tugs, and dumped into the ocean waters about four miles out.

The methods of street cleaning were considered deplorable. Streets covered with horse dung and accumulated debris were swept without benefit of sprinklers, causing choking dust clouds. Refuse, including rotting food, was tossed carelessly into open carts, much of it lost as the carts bumped along the irregularly surfaced streets. Ash barrels and garbage receptacles also were emptied into carts, causing more dust clouds and noxious odors. Although residents were instructed precisely when and where to put out their ash and garbage cans, and warned not to fill them to the brim, these often sat all day at the edge of the streets, causing an even worse stench. A severe rain or snow storm only magnified the predicament.

Perhaps an even more important public works function was the supply of water. The early eighties were the driest years ever recorded in the Croton watershed of Westchester and Putnam Counties since the opening of the Croton system in 1842. By 1883, the New York City administration had to conclude that neither the Croton aqueduct nor the city's reservoirs could meet the needs of the population any longer. Brooklyn, whose reservoir on the hill at Ridgewood depended on Long Island's streams for its water supply, was also experiencing a severe water shortage. While the Ridgewood distribution system had been in operation since 1859, there were hundreds of old wells of dubious purity still in use. In addition to the terrible shortage of water, waste of water was universal, and new, often faulty, plumbing resulted in an even worse situation. The most serious problem caused by the water shortage was the grave danger it posed to fire-fighting. The inadequate water pressure in hydrants along with the increasing heights of buildings combined to exacerbate the peril.

During 1883, both cities developed plans to expand their reservoirs and aqueducts. The plan for Brooklyn included extending conduits eastward through Long Island, tapping additional streams, and doubling the size of the Ridgewood reservoir, but it was still in its proposal stage at the end of '83. New York's plan involved heavier use of the Croton watershed. In June, the State Legislature voted to establish an autonomous Aqueduct Commission to lay out and construct a new aqueduct, with its necessary reservoirs and dams.

The presence of the state and federal governments in the cities was especially evident in immigration, military, and postal matters. The federal government empowered the State to oversee the entry of foreigners; the State operated the emigrant depot at Castle Garden as well as several hospitals on Ward's and Randall's Islands. The federal re-

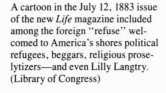
A cartoon in the July 12, 1883 issue of the new *Life* magazine included among the foreign "refuse" welcomed to America's shores political refugees, beggars, religious proselytizers—and even Lilly Langtry. (Library of Congress)

striction of Chinese entering the country had taken effect, and in '82, Congress had passed another act excluding the entry of those it labeled "undesirables," and had imposed a fifty-cent head tax on all arrivals.

Both the state and federal governments were active in the military. The New York State National Guard was seeking appropriations to build additional armories in both cities. The Seventh Regiment was all settled in its new building at Fourth Avenue and 66th Street. The U.S. Army had its regional headquarters on Governor's Island and maintained a series of harbor defenses, including Forts Hamilton and Lafayette at the southwest shore of Kings County. The Navy Yard in Brooklyn was still the largest facility of its kind in the nation, employing 2,000, although its activities had decreased since the War.

One of the least criticized government operations was the postal service, under the federal Post Office Department. Brooklyn's letter carriers delivered almost thirty-three million letters annually. The general Post Office on Washington Street, four branch offices, and 500 lamp-post boxes amply served the city's needs. Mail was picked up between five and seven times a day and delivered between two and four times.

New York's eight-year-old general Post Office, at the southern end of City Hall Park, had already become a popular landmark. The city had nineteen substations and 1,000 lamp-post boxes. Mail was collected below 59th on the east side and 70th on the west side on the average of sixteen times a day, and north of that on the average of six times daily and two or three times on Sunday. The mail was carried by wagon and on the els. To encourage even greater use of the mails and to wipe out a surplus in revenue, in October 1883 the Post Office dropped the postage on domestic letters from three to two cents.

The harsh manner of the immigration officers was a grievous surprise.
. . . As contrasted with the officials of my despotic country, those of the republic had been portrayed in my mind as paragons of refinement.
. . . These unfriendly voices flavored all America with a spirit of icy inhospitality that sent a chill through my very soul.

—Abraham Cahan

City Politics

While William Marcy Tweed was alive and in control of New York's Democratic Party organization, Tammany Hall, he would often dare his opposition to expose him. Only in the mid-1870s was the "Tweed Ring" crushed and Tweed himself imprisoned. Widespread graft and corruption had not been conducted with quite the same finesse since Tweed's day, but the patronage, vote-buying, bribery, collusion, and other tactics were carried out with sufficient fervor. Mayor Franklin Edson was basically a Tammany man, although he had been nominated

Just before election day, 1882, political cartoonist Thomas Nast warned the voter to "Look before you leap," as the Tammany "tiger" lay in wait below. (*Harper's Weekly*, November 4, 1882; Brooklyn Public Library)

Nast's comment on Mayor Edson's acquiescence to the Tammany "Indian," John Kelly. (*Harper's Weekly*, January 20, 1883; Brooklyn Public Library)

by a coalition of Tammany and County Democracy men. The County Democracy had been formed in 1880 by a group of wealthy Democrats—Congressman Abram Hewitt, his brother-in-law, ex-Mayor Edward Cooper, *Staats-Zeitung* publisher Oswald Ottendorfer, and financier and lawyer William C. Whitney among them. Organized as a counterweight to Tammany, it endeavored to limit both Tammany's control over party nominations and the power of its district leaders. But Edson's efforts to please all sides often failed. After fighting off repeated intimidation by Tammany boss "Honest John" Kelly, Edson gave in and appointed one of the machine's mainstays, Richard Croker, whom Kelly had called "one of the noblest works of God," as a fire commissioner.[9]

Brooklyn Mayor Seth Low appeared to be at the opposite extreme. Low, whose father had made a fortune in the China trade, was firmly Republican and firmly for good, responsible government. When he arrived at City Hall in 1882 at the age of thirty-two, the State Legislature had just granted Brooklyn a new charter, giving its mayor substantial authority over the various city departments. Low made full use of the new charter, appointing men on the basis of qualification rather than patronage and instituting long-needed reforms in administration.

The fall of 1883 marked another mayoral election for Brooklyn. Low was easily renominated as the Republican candidate in early October. To defeat Low, the Democrats needed a virtuous, creditable opponent. Hardly a lackey of Democratic boss Hugh McLaughlin, Joseph C. Hendrix, an editor of the *New York Sun* and a member of the Brooklyn Board of Education, would make such a formidable challenger. The Democratic mayoral nominating convention held at the Music Hall on Fulton and Flatbush in mid-October had been one of the largest gatherings Brooklyn had ever seen. Hendrix campaigned much as Low had in '81, on a platform of honest government run on business principles. Low, of course, ran on his record, claiming that his administration had been refreshingly free of the kind of patronage that had despoiled the office in earlier years. The Republicans spread rumors that the thirty-two-year-old Hendrix had been a Confederate general, and besides, did not pay his taxes. The Democrats made accusations that Low's non-partisan stance was a sham, and that, in fact, his appointments betrayed the fact that he was merely removing Democrats and replacing them with members of his own party. Toward the last days of the campaign, Brooklyn's most influential paper, the *Eagle*, grew sour on the Mayor, but two prominent figures, Reverend Henry Ward Beecher and Carl Schurz, the leading editor of New York's *Evening Post*, spoke on his behalf in glowing terms. In the end, on November 6th, Low won the election with just fifty-one percent of the vote.

Mayor Low was in the forefront of the movement toward good government and reform which marked the early eighties. Following the widespread political scandals that pervaded politics in the seventies from the national to the local levels, an anti-machine mood set in. One obvious area for the reformers to begin to tackle was civil service. In early 1883, President Chester A. Arthur, whose past was riddled with clubhouse politics, found himself signing the country's first civil service law, called the Pendleton Act. Its aim was to institute a system of government service at the federal level that would be based upon merit rather than political affiliation. In early 1883, a bill similar to the Pendleton Act, but for State employees, was introduced in the New York State Legislature. One section gave mayors of cities over 50,000 the authority to institute rules and examinations for government employees, although the areas of their jurisdiction were narrow. At the same time, the Legislature was considering a series of charter amendments for New York City, and asked Mayor Edson to present his suggestions. One month later, he submitted recommendations for limited civil service reform. Edson proposed to establish single heads of each administrative department and to grant the Mayor power to appoint and remove them.

Both the State civil service bill and the Mayor's charter amendment plan stimulated considerable debate. Recognizing an opportunity for getting some attention, the young reformer, Assemblyman Theodore Roosevelt, put forth a list of substantially more progressive charter amendments for the city. Although only twenty-five and in just his second term, the outspoken and ambitious assemblyman learned fast, and had pushed an impressive number of bills through the Legislature. Predicting that the charter amendments would get bogged down in debate, in early April he proposed a stronger set of civil service regulations that would pertain only to New York City.

In accepting the Democratic nomination for mayor of Brooklyn, Joseph C. Hendrix declared that his crusade would launch the Presidential campaign of 1884. (*Harper's Weekly*, November 3, 1883; Brooklyn Public Library)

Brooklyn Mayor Seth Low. (Henry R. Stiles, *History . . . of the County of Kings*, 1884; The Long Island Historical Society)

In May, the State civil service reform bill—including the section pertaining to large cities—became law, while Roosevelt's proposal was dismissed rather quickly. He was proved partially correct, however. At the end of the year, the Legislature was still debating the charter amendments.

Theodore Roosevelt . . . is the admitted leader of the republican forces in the Assembly. . . . He might have greater weight . . . but for his impulsiveness. . . . A peculiarity of his delivery is that in the rush of his words, his teeth suddenly lock together, and the effect is to mar his best efforts.

—The *New York Herald*

Studio portrait of the young Theodore Roosevelt, dressed for one of his favorite pursuits: ranching. (Library of Congress)

Urban Underpinnings

As fast as the cities were granting permits, private utility companies were installing the newest equipment for lighting, heating, telegraphing, and telephoning. The gas companies were continually installing street lamps and connections to houses and apartments. While the five major companies received permits to lay mains in forty-five streets in '83, they feared that soon electricity was going to take command. Even in Brooklyn and the rest of Kings County, where electric light was installed in stores and public buildings only on an isolated basis, the half-dozen gas companies were talking of consolidation as a protective course. Each of the 128 electric arc street lamps in Manhattan replaced between six and seven gas lamps, which worried the gas compnies even more. In spite of the opinion that electric lighting was more costly than gas, everyone realized that electricity gave off much more light. At the end of 1883, the City of Brooklyn finally granted a franchise to the Electric Illuminating Company of Brooklyn.

The New York City Department of Public Works issued permits to the Edison Electric Illuminating Company to lay underground conduits on twenty-two streets during 1883. Thomas Edison was working out of an Edison Company office at 65 Fifth Avenue, where, with the use of a small steam-powered electric generator, he was promoting a variety of his incandescent lamps and multiple-lamp ceiling fixtures, which he called electraliers. Edison was living in a hotel on Gramercy Park and working on improving the system of electrical transmission and distribu-

Utilities

Thomas Alva Edison, at the time he was working to bring electricity to New York City. (U.S. Department of the Interior, National Park Service, Edison National Historic Site)

Edison's threaded-base lamps and ornate centerpiece with four lamps. (James Dredge, *Electric Illumination*, 1885; Rutgers, the State University of New Jersey, Thomas A. Edison Papers)

THE N.Y. & BROOKLYN BRIDGE.
LIGHTED BY
70 WESTON ELECTRIC LIGHTS.
FURNISHED BY
THE UNITED STATES
ELECTRIC LIGHTING CO.
59 & 61 LIBERTY ST.   NEW YORK.

For its trade card, the Weston company employed what it felt to be its greatest achievement: the lighting of the Brooklyn Bridge. (Museum of the City of New York)

Press in the button and turn the crank *once only*; unhook the listening telephone (receiver) and put it close to your ear, when Central Office will inquire: "What number?" Give *Central Office and number* of person wanted, and upon receiving the answer "All right," hang up the receiver, and wait til your bell rings, then place the receiver to your ear and address person called.

—Instructions on how to
  place a telephone call

tion as well as trying to interest backers in establishing other central stations, similar to his station on Pearl Street in lower Manhattan. In addition to J.P. Morgan, Henry Villard and the Western Union Company also held a considerable interest in the Edison Company. From the original fifty-nine customers in September 1882, the company had grown to claim 500 just one year later. By the end of '83, the Pearl Street station had reached its capacity, and there was talk in the Edison office of a second district in the vicinity of Madison Square.

When the Brooklyn Bridge opened in May, it was lighted, not by the incandescent lamps of the Edison Electric Illuminating Company, but by seventy of the much brighter Weston arc lamps of the United States Illuminating Company. Back in February, the bridge trustees had approved the Weston company's low bid over those of Edison and Brush.

The telegraph had become so prevalent by 1883 that it was hard to find any place left where new service was required. Jay Gould's Western Union Company operated 400,000 miles of wire that extended throughout the country. Having survived the national strike of the telegrapher's union, the company's future prosperity seemed insured.

In 1883, there were some 4,500 telephones in service in New York, and new telephones could not be installed fast enough. Most of the subscribers of the Metropolitan Telephone and Telegraph Company and the Long Island Telephone Company were businesses—Cooper, Hewitt & Co., Drexel, Morgan & Co., in New York, and Pratt Manufacturing and Ovington Bros. in Brooklyn—and the 16,000 daily calls made were primarily for business purposes. Non-subscribers could make calls to subscribers at several dozen public telegraph offices.

With the rapid expansion of utilities, the overwhelming numbers of poles and overhead wires and underground tubes for telegraph, telephone, and electricity were creating havoc on the city streets. In early January, for example, workers for one company were erecting poles to carry electric wires on the south side of 40th Street opposite the old reservoir. Local residents protested rather vociferously, and the confrontation resulted in several arrests on both sides. Although the company was enjoined from continuing its work, the issue was, by no means, resolved. And on top of all this, the Fire Department complained to Mayor Edson that all the wires were interfering with the city's fire alarm telegraph apparatus.

In 1883, the State Legislature was scheduled to pass a bill requiring that telegraph and telephone wires be placed underground, a measure that was thought to be the only practical solution. Western Union asserted that by mid-'83 it would have placed underground all of the 2,000 wires entering its building on Broadway. A major difficulty in all of the efforts was that no method had been found to insulate the wires adequately. One insulating material, gutta-percha, thought to be the best available, was found to melt at the slightest rise in temperature.

The various utility companies met to discuss possible ways of placing their wires under the streets, and, if possible, for installing them in a single conduit. But the basically competitive enterprises could hardly be expected to cooperate in such a complex matter. The U.S. Illuminating Company, for example, found that when it was sued for mounting wires on West 43rd Street, the Edison Company was providing legal aid to the plaintiffs. In one of its last acts of the year, the New York City Board of Aldermen voted to give the electric light companies two years to get their wires underground. The State Legislature still had not acted.

With the rapid growth of New York and Brooklyn, many changes were taking place in the ways people got about. There were dozens of ferries in the rivers and harbor, over a dozen between New York and Brooklyn alone. Several railroads came into Grand Central Depot, and there were also commuter and freight lines that used a terminal on the far west side. Rail lines from the west and south of the country terminated in New Jersey, from where one took a ferry to Manhattan or an "annex boat" directly to Brooklyn. The els stretched from one end of Manhattan to the other, and horse-car lines pervaded the streets of both cities. Construction of a railroad tunnel under the Hudson River, begun almost a decade earlier, had been suspended again in 1882 for lack of funds.

The major thoroughfare of New York was Broadway, and its lower end could not have been more congested. With traffic going every which way, the unfortunate pedestrian had little else to rely on but a sense of humor. As one story went, a farmer, asked why he was standing so long on one side of Broadway, replied, "I'm

The laying of underground wires by the Western Union Telegraph Company. (*Scientific American*, September 29, 1883; Brooklyn Public Library)

Getting In, Out, and Around

The brakemen and conductors . . . are so learned they never speak English. . . . They never say "Forty-second-street" or "Chatham-Square". . . . When they announce "Ntysvsteet" or "Chamskare" . . . they are only talking in their usual elevated style. Don't imagine you can understand them, because you can't. They don't intend that you shall.

—Tips for tourists
  taking the elevateds

A traffic jam on lower Broadway; St. Paul's Chapel is on the left and the general Post Office is in the background. (*Harper's Weekly*, December 29, 1883; Brooklyn Public Library)

jes' waiting for the parade to pass by." And another quip told of a sea captain who confessed, "I'd sooner cross the Atlantic in a raging storm than try to make my way across Broadway." New Yorkers prided themselves on their pedestrian daring, and on how few accidents actually occurred.

During 1883, some 93 million persons traveled on Manhattan's elevated railroads. Jay Gould was leasing the two existing elevated companies under the single management of the Manhattan Railway Company. Along with Russell Sage and Cyrus Field, Gould had been heavily involved in their initial financing. On the west side, the Ninth Avenue El ran from the South Ferry at the Battery up to 155th and Eighth Avenue at the Harlem River. The Sixth Avenue line ran from South Ferry up to West 53rd Street, where it turned west to join with the Ninth Avenue line. The Third Avenue line ran from South Ferry to 129th and the river, and at 42nd Street had a spur to Grand Central. The Second Avenue line ran from Chatham Square, where one could transfer from the Third Avenue, up to 127th and the river. It also had a spur, running east on 34th Street to the ferry to Long Island City. The next move, of course, would be the extension north into the Annexed District.

The fare on the els was ten cents except between 5:30 and 8:30 a.m. and 4:30 and 7:30 p.m.—called "commission hours"—when it was reduced to five cents, presumably to benefit the working classes traveling to and from their places of employment. During those hours, the already packed trains were all the more jammed because of

The Ninth Avenue Elevated curving through a still rural section of Manhattan, at 110th Street. (Library of Congress)

65

the reduced rates. In early '83, the State Legislature approved a uniform five-cent fare at all times, and sent the measure to the Governor. Gould's associates were incensed, arguing that the reduction would do the unthinkable—preclude the company's distribution of adequate dividends to the stockholders. (The railway's actual profits were a mystery, since the company refused to release any figures.) Perceiving the lower fare as an ideal political issue, Tammany Hall came out strongly in its favor. Governor Cleveland, however, waited to act until the last minute. He felt pressured by the business community to defy the Legislature and maintain the ten-cent fare; in any case, whatever remaining ties he had with Tammany were almost severed. But he did not want to disappoint the public. Commerce prevailed: on March 2nd, the last day he could respond, Cleveland vetoed the bill.

As if to inflame the already existing ire of the elevated passengers, the Manhattan Railway announced that as of January, trains on the Sixth Avenue line would cease running between midnight and 5:30 a.m. The Second and Ninth Avenue lines already shut down at 8:00, and only the Third Avenue ran after 12:00. Because, the company claimed, so few traveled during those hours, it was losing money. Riders grumbled that evening events would be impossible to attend, and that cab fares were prohibitive. Gould was heard to have mumbled that only the dissipated took trains at night.

The steam-powered elevated trains experienced fairly frequent accidents, often derailings. They were noisy, gritty, and dirty, but the rider could not help but be thrilled to speed along up in the air, whizzing by the busy city below. The el, after all, was still a novelty.

The most common form of transit in the two cities was the horse car. Running on iron rails and pulled by a single horse, each could seat about thirty people. Manhattan had thirty-two lines in '83. Believing that it would harm their business, the Broadway shopkeepers had blocked a line from coming all the way down their thoroughfare, but everyone knew that one was inevitable. Most rides cost five cents. Brooklyn had fourteen horse-car lines, which carried about 93 million passengers annually; Manhattan's thirty-two carried nearly 120 million.

In addition, the streets of the two cities were jammed with a wide assortment of omnibuses, or stages, carriages, hackneys, and wagons. Although the horse-car

Financier Jay Gould. (*Harper's Weekly*, March 18, 1882; Brooklyn Public Library)

The idea that a corporation after obtaining . . . a valuable franchise . . . should adopt the policy of serving the public only in such hours of the day as were profitable is a revelation to many who have not fully comprehended the greed, arrogance, and assurance of the . . . railroad managers.

—*The New York Times*

lines had pretty much taken over the omnibus routes by '83, there were still several omnibus lines—on Broadway, Ninth Avenue, and Madison Avenue. A well-traveled route in Brooklyn ran from the Brooklyn side of the Wall Street ferry out Lafayette to Classon Avenue. Prosperous Brooklynites also relied heavily on cabs. In the beginning of May, new and larger cabs of bright yellow, drawn by two horses, appeared on Montague Street. There was talk of installing a cable car to run up Montague from the ferry, but local residents, such as Henry Pierrepont, were raising a vigorous opposition.

With the May opening of the Brooklyn Bridge, the demand for elevated lines increased greatly. The local press ridiculed Brooklyn's "leading citizens," who, one critic charged, would get together every once in a while to declare that "rapid transit is an absolute necessity," but then do nothing about it.[10] At the end of December, the Kings County Elevated Railroad Company was granted a franchise to complete an elevated line from Fulton Ferry out to Bedford.

The great bridge was proving to be a popular tourist attraction. In its first seven months, more than four million people walked across, and between September and December, one million rode across on the new cable railway. The ferry companies feared a disastrous decline in ridership as a result. There was some decline, and Pierrepont's Union Ferry Company announced a slight reduction of some of its fares in June, but the companies were far from going out of business.

In the 1860s, William H. Vanderbilt's father, "Commodore" Cornelius Vanderbilt, who had made a fortune in shipping, had moved into land transportation and quickly gained control of the railroads directly connecting New York with Buffalo and Chicago. At Fourth Avenue and 42nd Street—the point at which law prohibited steam trains from going farther south—a locomotive house and several other railroad buildings had been constructed.

In order to accommodate a growing number of passengers, Vanderbilt planned a grand depot to stretch along 42nd Street and Vanderbilt Avenue and hired the architect J.B. Snook, who would adapt a variety of the most fashionable European styles, to design it. Behind the imposing red brick facade trimmed in white, Grand Central Depot concealed an enormous arched iron and glass train shed 652 feet long, 200 feet wide, and 100 feet high.

The Brooklyn Bridge has now been open not quite five months. . . . Up to October 1, 1,865,800 persons passed over the bridge from New-York to Brooklyn, while only 1,519,600 came over . . . from Brooklyn to New-York. . . . At this rate New-York will be utterly depopulated in less than two years.

—*The New York Times*

About 125 trains arrived and departed daily, and the terminal could handle twelve trains at one time. From the north end of the train shed at 45th Street, four tracks ran north up Fourth Avenue—first through a yard at street level, then into a tunnel, and then, north of 96th Street, over a stone viaduct across the Harlem flats. Iron bridges for carriages and pedestrians spanned the yard in the 40s, and to the north, openings cut into the tunnel allowed the engines' smoke to escape. There were stations—in effect, commuter stations—either below or above grade at 60th, 73rd, 86th, 110th, and 126th Streets.

Many had ridiculed Vanderbilt for erecting such an elaborate depot so far from the center of town—a full forty-five minute horse-car ride from City Hall. But the Commodore was right. By 1883, the city had moved north, and society had moved north along with it.

The only contemporary form of transportaton that New York lacked was the underground railway. In 1883 there was some talk about building one. The Broadway Underground Railway Company had been established and was preparing a feasibility study for an underground line, similar to that in London, which would run from one end of Manhattan to the other.

Vanderbilt's Grand Central Depot, looking east along 42nd Street. (Museum of the City of New York)

From Cradle to Grave

Observing the Faith

Without any question, the best known religious figure in the two cities—if not the country—was Henry Ward Beecher. The pastor of Brooklyn's Plymouth Church since 1847, he had triumphed as an orator on the issue of slavery, functioned successfully as his own self-promoter, and survived a lengthy and entangled personal scandal. In 1883, Beecher was celebrating his seventieth birthday and the thirty-sixth anniversary of his pastorate at Plymouth. At the fete given in his honor at the Academy of Music in June, every important Brooklyn citizen was present, even Democratic boss Hugh McLaughlin. Cheers filled the house not only for the preacher, but, at the mention of *Uncle Tom's Cabin*, for his sister, Harriet Beecher Stowe. Beecher was still considered a daring figure, allowing a black minister to preach from his pulpit and lending his name—for a fee—for commercial advertising.

Without a doubt, the region's loudest and most flamboyant religious figure also hailed from Brooklyn. T. De Witt Talmage presided over what was claimed to be the largest Protestant church in the country, the Tabernacle Presbyterian Church on Schermerhorn Street. When a devastating fire destroyed the previous church, Talmage was heard to exclaim that it was a magnificent opportunity to build an even bigger church, one that would hold 5,000 congregants, 2,000 more than before.

Compared with Beecher and Talmage, who themselves vied for the attention of a devoted press, the rest of the two cities' religious personages paled. In Manhattan, Grace Church at Broadway and 10th was the patrician of the Episcopal churches, and, next to Trinity Church downtown, the wealthiest. Manhattan and Brooklyn pos-

The Bloomingdale Reformed Church at West 71st and Ninth Avenue; the Dakota Apartments at 72nd and Eighth Avenue are seen on the right. (Museum of the City of New York)

sessed numerous other Episcopal churches for society, such as Holy Trinity in the Heights in Brooklyn, and St. Thomas on New York's Fifth Avenue, with its impressive interiors by John La Farge and Augustus Saint-Gaudens. The equally fashionable St. Bartholomew's at Madison and 44th was known to undertake considerable charity work among the poor of the east side. Uptown, at Madison and 71st, a new building for St. James was going up.

For one Protestant church, 1883 meant rebirth. The breakup of the old estates, and the proliferation of squatters dislocated by the construction of Central Park, resulted in a general decline of the west side—as the *Times* put it, the area was given up to "shanties and goats."[11] Because of this decline, one of New York's oldest churches —the Bloomingdale Reformed—had lost much of its congregation. But now, with the convenience of the el and with all the building activity, exemplified by the Dakota, the existing church at 71st and Ninth Avenue was proving inadequate to the community's needs. In '83, the church announced that a new building would rise at 68th Street.

The urbanizing communities of Brooklyn were also providing expanding congregations for that city's churches. The growing neighborhood west of Prospect Park dedicated two churches in '83, both at Seventh Avenue and St. Johns Place. Both of the congregations—at Grace Methodist Episcopal Church and at the Memorial Presbyterian Church—had outgrown their existing chapels.

The two cities had innumerable houses of worship that served an increasing variety of congregations. The Roman Catholic Church probably constituted the largest non-Protestant sect. In Manhattan there were some sixty Catholic churches, serving a broad array of populations, from the Catholic elite who attended the new St. Patrick's to the far more humble Irish of the 4th Ward, who went to St. James's, north of the new Brooklyn Bridge. The newest arrivals from Poland attended St. Stanislaus on Stanton Street. Brooklyn's Bishop John Loughlin used Brooklyn's St. James's Church on Jay Street as his cathedral, but it was his greatest hope to complete a larger edifice for the Brooklyn Diocese out on Lafayette Avenue.

The black population of each city had its own set of religious institutions. In Brooklyn the larger black churches included the Bridge Street African Wesleyan Episcopal Church and the Fleet Street Bethel Methodist

The new—and still spireless—St. Patrick's Cathedral, taken from Fifth Avenue and 51st Street. (Museum of the City of New York)

Reverend William Spellman, Minister of the Abyssinian Baptist Church. (Abyssinian Baptist Church)

Episcopal Church downtown, and the Bethel African Methodist Episcopal in Bedford. The Zion AME Church in the Eastern District had dedicated a new building in early '83 on South 3rd. In Manhattan, the more prominent black churches included the Abyssinian Baptist Church, the AME Bethel, and the new St. Benedict Roman Catholic Church, all south of Washington Square, and the Shiloh Presbyterian on West 26th Street.

The German-Jewish and older Sephardic populations of New York were associated generally with the more established synagogues. The Sephardim attended the Spanish-Portuguese synagogue, Shearith Israel, at its newest building on West 19th Street. German Jews attended the Reform Temple Emanu-El, an imposing Moorish edifice designed by Leopold Eidlitz at Fifth Avenue and 43rd Street, or Ahawath Chesed at Lexington and 55th. The oldest Ashkenazic congregation, B'nai Jeshurun, was on 34th Street, just west of Broadway. Downtown, a whole new group of Eastern European Orthodox congregations was forming, although Beth Hamidrash on Allen Street had been founded back in 1852. Brooklyn's synagogues included the Congregation of Beth Israel downtown, Temple Israel on Greene Avenue, which conducted Reform services in English, and Temple Beth Jacob in the Eastern District.

Many other religious organizations served the cities' enormous variety of ethnic groups, including the Chinese Methodist Episcopal Mission on Mott, the Italian Mission on Leonard, the Hungarian Presbyterian Mission

Fifth Avenue, looking north from 43rd Street; Temple Emanu-El is on the right. (Museum of the City of New York)

71

on 2nd, the Santiago Episcopal Church on West 14th, the Gustavus Adolphus Swedish Lutheran Church on East 22nd, and the German Baptist Church in Washington Heights.

New York's public institutions were administered under three Commissioners of Public Charities and Corrections. The largest collection of these was located on Blackwell's Island in the East River. A series of somber granite buildings held the charity hospital, the lunatic asylum, the almshouse, the workhouse, the blind asylum, the hospital for incurables, the convalescent hospital, and the penitentiary. Each of these suffered from varying degrees of overcrowding and generally deteriorating conditions. The lunatic asylum, however, was beginning to receive some attention for its modern methods; as the *Times* noted, the "tendency of treatment is largely in the direction of less physical restraint."[12] Brooklyn and Kings County had a considerably smaller array of public charity institutions.

The annual report of the New York City Mission and Tract Society for the year 1883 listed nearly 500 charity organizations throughout the twenty-four wards of New York. Each year, the problem of poverty in the two cities was becoming more serious. Those in charge of the charity institutions separated the poor into two groups: the deserving poor, those who struggled and suffered through no fault of their own, and the undeserving poor, those who thrived on the dole, or simply became hopelessly dependent. They believed aid to the poor was essential, both for providing society with a sense of moral uplift and for controlling potential social unrest in the slums.

During the Tweed era, Tammany's control over the administration of public charity had resulted in large-scale corruption. It was thought that one way to stop the political control over charity was to limit public authority. In the late seventies, both cities suspended those areas of public assistance which had provided clothing, food, coal, and even money to thousands of residents annually. While the public charity boards in each city and the State continued to oversee the asylums, hospitals, and other institutions for those deemed indigent, insane, and criminal, and in limited degrees to provide individual assistance, a good deal of responsibility for assisting the poor was being transferred to the private organization.

Assisting the Poor

Were it not the home of criminals and paupers Blackwell's Island would probably be dotted with the mansions of our millionaires.

—*The New York Times*

Ignorant alms-giving, which is simply indolent self-indulgence, teaches that skillful lying and laziness can get more money in a day than honest labor.

—*Harper's Weekly*

The private philanthropic groups took up the burden with great determination. It seemed as if new charity groups were forming every day, and some kind of coordinating body seemed imperative. After much ground work, the Charity Organization Society (COS) of New York was founded in 1882, not only to coordinate the activities of the many existing organizations, but also to avoid the inevitable duplication of services and to provide for the painstaking investigation of those who applied for assistance. Among the larger private Manhattan charities were the New York Association for Improving the Condition of the Poor, the Children's Aid Society, the Young Men's and Young Women's Christian associations, the Young Men's Hebrew Association, the Colored Orphan Asylum, the Hebrew Orphan Asylum, the Association Fraterna Italiana, the Lutheran Emigrant Home, and the United Hebrew Charities.

Even with fewer private aid societies than New York, Brooklyn conducted its charity work with equal fervor. Seth Low, who had been instrumental in restricting public assistance in Brooklyn, was heavily involved in its reorganization. Along with philanthropists such as A.T. White and Darwin James, Low organized the Brooklyn Bureau of Charities in 1879 to coordinate the efforts of the various private groups and to reduce the chances of duplicating aid. A registry of acceptable clients was compiled; in 1883 some 5,150 were listed. The Bureau's work was organized according to districts, to which "friendly visitors" were assigned. The friendly visitor, advised not to "announce yourself as a visitor . . . but as a friend or neighbor who has heard of their troubles," took pride in uncovering the fraudulent husband or the unscrupulous widow.[13] Among the private societies working with the Bureau were the Women's Work Exchange and Employment Society of Brooklyn, the Brooklyn Children's Aid Society, the Brooklyn Society for the Prevention of Cruelty to Children, the Young Men's Christian Association, the Christian Union for Chinese Work, the Howard Colored Orphan Asylum, and the Hebrew Orphan Asylum of Brooklyn.

Maintaining the Health

As knowledge about the causes and cures of disease increased, so did the public assumption of responsibility toward maintaining standards of health. Yellow fever, cholera, consumption, typhus, and diptheria caused great fear among the general populace. More and more, urban residents were warned to be meticulous in the purchase and preparation of food.

The city and State maintained large facilities on Blackwell's, Ward's, and Randall's Islands for both curing and isolating the ill. The largest public hospital in Manhattan was Bellevue, at the foot of East 26th Street. When the city announced in 1883 that it would build a new hospital for the confinement of those with contagious diseases, referred to as a "fever hospital," in a tenement area at the foot of East 16th Street, local residents raised a furor. Among New York's many private hospitals were St. Vincent's on West 11th Street, which was building a new wing at 12th and Seventh Avenue, the New York Medical College and Hospital for Women, farther uptown, and Mt. Sinai Hospital on Lexington and 66th Street.

While New York's death rate was almost 26 per 1,000 population in 1883, the Brooklyn Board of Health was priding itself on a death rate of just over 22 per 1,000, a drop of two points from 1882. Brooklyn's public hospital, the Brooklyn Hospital, just east of downtown, served all those in need regardless of color or nationality.

Among Brooklyn's private medical institutions was the Long Island College Hospital on Pacific Street, which included, in addition to its hospital, a dispensary, a medical school, and a training school for nurses. An all-female board administered the Women's Dispensary and Hospital at DeKalb Avenue near Debevoise, which had been founded in 1881 to serve primarily poor women and children. The new building of the Eastern District Hospital and Dispensary at South 3rd, which had been scheduled to open by early '83, was experiencing extensive problems. The most serious was that the building was so large and airy that no one quite knew how to heat it. And on a much smaller and more personal scale, Sister Elisabeth Fedde, an Oslo-trained Lutheran nursing deaconess, responded to a call by Norwegian settlers in Brooklyn and arrived in the U.S. in 1883 to establish a small nursing station in Red Hook.

Just as the two cities' departments of Charities and Corrections dealt with assisting the poor and maintaining the health, so they took responsibility for the punishment of the lawbreaker. The conditions of the facilities they maintained for these purposes, however, were deplorable. And although the press did not treat the criminal with

Efficacious as M. Pasteur's rules [for the prevention of cholera] doubtless are, most people will decide that it would be preferable to die of cholera rather than to try to live under the conditions prescribed.

—*The New York Times*

Punishing the Criminal

much compassion, it doted on condemning prison conditions. The Tombs in Lower Manhattan, the Penitentiary on Blackwell's Island, and the House of Refuge for juveniles on Randall's Island were the subject of numerous articles, censuring them as hovels not fit for human life. Adjacent to downtown Brooklyn, the Kings County Jail on Raymond Street was housed in a fairly new facility, and had not yet had a chance to be the brunt of disapproval. The Kings County Penitentiary, near the Brooklyn-Flatbush border, was situated too far out to receive much attention of any kind.

Burying the Dead

As the cities' populations jumped, so did the number and size of their cemeteries. The old cemeteries of lower Manhattan, such as the Jewish burial grounds and the churchyards of Trinity and St. Paul's, had become historical landmarks. A number of cemeteries were established in Queens and Kings counties to serve the various religious denominations of the region.

For many decades, society of New York and Brooklyn had buried their dead in the majestic Green-Wood Cemetery at the edge of the City of Brooklyn. Some 24,000 lots had been sold by '83, and some 217,000 bodies interred. By the early eighties, Woodlawn in the Annexed District was becoming the cemetery that society preferred.

Opportunities for Learning

The cities of New York and Brooklyn had extensive public education systems. The New York City Board of Education reported in 1883 that more than 290,000 children were attending 298 schools and colleges, instructed by 3,700 men and women. Attendance was compulsory for those between eight and fourteen years. There were forty-six grammar schools for older boys, forty-six for older girls, and eleven for both boys and girls; forty-five primary schools for younger children and sixty-eight primary departments within the grammar schools; three "colored" schools; forty-eight sundry industrial schools, reformatories, and orphan asylums; twenty-seven evening schools, and a nautical school on the *St. Mary's* at the foot of East 23rd Street.

In 1878, the New York City Board had declared that all schools were open to white and black students, in compliance with the State's Civil Rights Act of 1873. The Board, concluding that the black population still preferred separate schools, kept the black schools open. But by the beginning of '83, the attendance at the three colored schools had declined to such an extent that the Board considered closing them. As a result, several dozen black teachers and principals would lose their jobs.

With about 100,000 students enrolled in Brooklyn, the average daily attendance was slightly under 60,000. There were some sixty public schools, including the five-year-old Central Grammar School—Brooklyn's first upper-level school—on Court Street, and three colored schools. Slightly over 1,300 teachers were employed.

The Brooklyn Board had resisted the move toward desegregation, claiming that black parents desired separate schools where the needs and concerns of their children would be better understood. In 1882 Mayor Low appointed the first black member, Philip A. White, to the Board. By the end of '83 the Board adopted a formula for the admission of black students to regular schools while retaining the colored schools and their staffs for those pupils who chose to stay there. Colored School No. 2 in the Weeksville section of Bedford, for example, would be renumbered as a standard public school, but still continue as one for black pupils with black teachers and administration.

Women played a large but subordinate role in public education, occupying the relatively powerless and poorly paid positions. Many were teachers, and some were prin-

Getting an Education

The original Colored School No. 2 on Troy Avenue. (The Long Island Historical Society)

cipals of the primary schools, but very few ran any of the grammar schools, where pay was better. None served on either city's Board of Education.

Schools in both cities suffered from considerable overcrowding, lack of adequate ventilation, light, and heat, and unsanitary plumbing. To help address this situation, the health boards of each city were beginning to include data on the deteriorating school plants in their annual reports.

Brooklyn had another serious and long-debated problem, this one over the issue of free textbooks. Critics complained that public education was not really free as long as the Board did not appropriate money for free books. After much delay, Mayor Low announced that by the beginning of 1884, a uniform procedure for free textbooks would be initiated.

Both cities had innumerable private and parochial preparatory schools. To the south of downtown Brooklyn, for example, St. Francis College, under the aegis of the Brothers of the Order of St. Francis, was open to young men and boys, and was in the process of applying to the State for permission to confer college degrees. The Brooklyn Collegiate and Polytechnic Institute on Livingston Street served the young men of Brooklyn society, and the Packer Collegiate Institute on Joralemon served its young women. In '83, the burgeoning community west of Prospect Park established the Prospect Park Collegiate School for Girls in a brownstone on Lincoln Place. In Manhattan, the Rutgers Female College moved from its building on Fifth Avenue across from the reservoir and relocated up on West 55th. Trinity School in the West 40s was typical of the proper New York preparatory school for young gentlemen. St. James's Parochial School in the 4th Ward devoted itself to educating the neighborhood's Irish youth. The Workingman's School and Free Kindergarten of the Society for Ethical Culture, spearheaded by Felix Adler, was providing industrial training as well as ordinary instruction to deserving youth. The *Machzike Talmud Torah* opened in March 1883 on East Broadway and offered after-school instruction in Hebrew.

Elocution medal, presented in 1883 to Alfred E. Smith at the St. James's School in the 4th Ward. (Museum of the City of New York)

Higher Education

New York seemed proud of the variety of its institutions of higher learning, but an outsider might have been somewhat disappointed at their number. The New York

City Board of Education ran two public colleges. The College of the City of New York at Lexington and 23rd was open to young males from the city and offered classical and scientific courses and a post-graduate course in engineering. The class of '83 had forty-nine graduates in the undergraduate and Masters courses. The Normal College for young women at 69th and Lexington trained students as public school teachers; the class of 1883 contained 239 students.

New York University, flanking the east side of Washington Square. (New York University Archives)

Private institutions included the rapidly growing Columbia College at Madison and 49th. It offered four-year and graduate courses to males in its schools of Arts, Mines, Law, Political Science, and Medicine. The University of the City of New York—now being referred to as New York University—contained departments of arts, science, including a school of art, and law at its Washington Square building, and a medical college that was up near Bellevue Hospital. The Women's Medical College on the east side was associated with the New York Infirmary for Women and Children. And Manhattan College on the Boulevard in Manhattanville was a prominent Catholic institution that was operated by the Christian Brothers.

New York's colleges, for the most part, were male bastions. Three women, however, had been enrolled in New York University's School of Art in 1873-74. The issue of wider admission of women at NYU had come up as early as 1876, and the administration decided that as long

The NYU class of 1883, the school's fiftieth commencement. (New York University Archives)

Women's engraving class at the Cooper Union. (*Frank Leslie's Illustrated Newspaper,* April 14, 1883; Brooklyn Public Library)

as no cost to the university would be involved, the determination could be left to the faculty.

A move to admit women to Columbia College gained momentum in '83. At the time, however, Columbia's Board of Trustees was more concerned with developing a strategy to transform the school into a national university. In June, the Board expressed its general approval of the education of women, but not at Columbia. The idea of an "annex" to Columbia was raised but quickly dropped. In the end, the Trustees voted to allow women to take the equivalent of an entrance exam which could qualify them either to matriculate—not at Columbia, but at a school which admitted women—or to pursue a non-resident course leading to a non-degree certificate. Opposed to the concept of an annex for women, and predicting that this final plan was doomed to fail, Columbia's President, Frederick A.P. Barnard, had been campaigning for complete co-education.

New York's art schools included the Art Students' League near Union Square, open to professional artists and to skilled men and women who intended to pursue art as a career. About 1,200 students were enrolled in the Cooper Union's art classes, about half of whom were attending its Women's Art School.

A number of societies, such as the New York Academy of Medicine and the New York Bar Association, had formed to advance various professional relationships. The American Society of Civil Engineering, for example, recently had celebrated its thirtieth birthday. And the New

York Academy of Sciences was meeting on Monday evenings at Columbia's Hamilton Hall.

The Library

What the two cities lacked in formal institutions of higher learning, they compensated for in libraries—just as long as one could afford the necessary annual fees and had the proper credentials. New York's Astor Library, on Lafayette Place, prided itself on having over 208,000 volumes and nearly 60,000 readers each year. The non-circulating library was open to any respectable individual from 9:00 to 5:00, to 4:00 in the winter. To suggestions that the Astor open for at least part of the evening, the trustees replied—mistakenly—that there was no precedent for this anywhere else in the world. The newer Lenox Library, on Fifth Avenue and 70th, was open even fewer hours than the Astor, and closed for the entire summer. Admission, obtained by writing to the superintendent, was known to be far more than a mere formality. The Harlem Library, the Mercantile Library, and the Apprentices' Library —the latter two intended for clerks and young workers— remained open until 9:00, but each of them required an annual fee.

Two free libraries were located in lower Manhattan. The Cooper Union's reading room was open in the evening as well as on Sundays and had some 2,000 users a day. The relatively new New York Free Circulating Library on Bond Street was founded by a group of women from Grace Church, who felt that none of the existing libraries really served the poor. A third institution, the Women's Library on Bleecker Street, was established by the Working Women's Protective Union with an annual fee of $1.50, which was waived for anyone unable to pay.

The city had many special libraries as well. The New York Academy of Sciences library of 6,000 volumes was housed at the American Museum of Natural History. And in a very different field, the music publisher, G. Schirmer, maintained a circulating library at its shop on Union Square.

Brooklyn had several large libraries. The Brooklyn Library, formerly the Mercantile Library, in an ornate Gothic-style building on Montague across from the Academy of Music, had some 80,000 volumes. For a year's subscription of five dollars, one had the use of two large reading rooms as well as circulating privileges. Its Eastern District Branch Library and Reading Room was opened in

The [Astor] library closes at 4 P.M. during the winter. Its hours effectively bar its use to business men and clerks, working students, and in fact to many hard workers in the profession of letters.

—*White, Stokes, & Allen's Guide and Select Directory*

80

In the early 1880s, the rear of the
Lenox Library still faced a hay field.
(Museum of the City of New York)

1882, and its subscribers could also use the Montague
Street facility.

The Brooklyn Institute of Arts and Sciences provided a library for young men, which was an outgrowth of
the 1823 Apprentices' Library. The YMCA on Fulton also
had a library open to young men. And by 1883, the Long
Island Historical Society, with its handsome reading
room, was well established in a new building designed by
George B. Post, on Pierrepont Street.

What People Were Reading

For his history of New York, Benson Lossing calcu-
lated that nearly 540 newspapers and magazines were being published in the city in 1883. There were 29 morning
dailies, 9 evening dailies, 10 semi-weeklies, 254 weeklies
(of which about 50 were religious), 36 bi-weeklies and
semi-monthlies, 185 monthlies, 3 bi-monthlies, and 11
quarterlies. Many of their offices lined Printing House
Square and Park Row opposite City Hall Park and the Post
Office.

The *New York Herald* was the leading paper, with a
daily circulation of 60,000. Its owner, James Gordon
Bennett, was the son of the paper's illustrious founder, the
distinguished publisher and journalist whose name he
bore. Whitelaw Reid's *Tribune* had some 35,000 readers.
Even with the great new suspension bridge looming up
over Printing House Square, the *Tribune's* red-brick
clock-towered structure, designed by Richard Morris
Hunt, was a prominent landmark of lower Manhattan.
The *Times*, the leading Republican journal, had a circulation similar to that of the *Tribune*. It celebrated its thirty-
second birthday by reducing the price of its daily edition
from four to two cents, declaring that the paper, which, it

said, was read by the wealthy "because of its excellence," should also be read by the poor "because of its cheapness."[14] With the elder Bennett's death and that of the *Tribune's* Horace Greeley, there was hardly a striking figure left in journalism, unless it was Charles A. Dana. Dana considered his *Sun* to be the paper of the working people and maintained that it was strictly independent.

In 1883, the *World* was in financial trouble, with a circulation only half that of the *Tribune* and the *Times*. On May 9, 1883, Joseph Pulitzer, the Hungarian immigrant who had made a name for himself in St. Louis, took over the *World* from its owner, Jay Gould, and proclaimed it would be the real paper of the working classes. The *Evening Post,* owned by Henry Villard, was considered the best of the evening papers, and was admired for its book reviews. Although the paper was thoroughly Republican, its editor, Carl Schurz, the German immigrant who had been a Republican U.S. Senator and Secretary of the Interior, became irrevocably opposed to its editorial policy, particularly its opposition to the telegraph strike. In December of 1883, he resigned.

The new editor of the *World,* Joseph Pulitzer. (*Harper's Weekly,* June 2, 1883; Brooklyn Public Library)

Every ethnic group seemed to have at least one newspaper. A new one for the Chinese community, *Chinese American,* had just appeared. The *Staats-Zeitung, Il Progresso Italo-Americano,* and the *Jewish Gazette* were several of the many that were available.

Brooklyn enjoyed a full complement of papers, a situation that was, perhaps, made all the more necessary by the anti-Brooklyn attitudes of the New York press—where coverage was reserved, or so it seemed, only for those Brooklyn residents unfortunate enough to be murdered or thrown in jail. The Brooklyn daily press included the *Eagle,* the *Times,* and the *Union.* Brooklyn's immigrant population also provided sufficient demand for a number of foreign-language journals, such as the *Freie Presse* and the *Stats Svenska Argus.* And one monthly, the *Brooklyn Advance,* focused on local events, the doings of society, fashion news, and popular literature.

New York's periodicals were particularly cosmopolitan, and included *Harper's Weekly* and *Harper's Monthly, Century, Puck, Frank Leslie's Illustrated Newspaper, North American Review, Scientific American,* the *Nation,* the *Home Journal,* and the *Police Gazette.* A new satirical journal, *Life,* began publication in 1883. *Demorest's Family Magazine* and *Harper's Bazar* were

There is room in the great and growing city for a journal that is not only cheap but bright, not only bright, but large, not only large but truly Democratic—dedicated to the cause of the people rather than that of purse-potentates.

—Editorial, the *New York World,* May 11, 1883

eagerly read by the matron who wanted to catch up on the latest fashions, or who was following the latest install-ment of a novel by Louisa M. Alcott or Thomas Hardy. A new breed of woman journalist, such as Mrs. Jane Cunningham Croly, who wrote under the name Jenny June in *Demorest's,* was reassessing the role of women both within and outside the home. *Demorest's, Peterson's Magazine,* the *Delineator* (published by E. Butterick & Company), and *Harper's Bazar* kept readers up-to-date on the current Paris styles, and sometimes included dressmaking patterns. One could follow the latest in fiction, and, at the same time, become more informed about the condition of women in society. The January 13th issue of *Harper's Bazar,* for example, included an article, "The Promise of the Dawn," that predicted an optimistic future for women.

In addition to Alcott and Hardy, the monthlies serial-ized many other current popular authors: Henry James, Mark Twain, Julia Ward Howe, Joel Chandler Harris, Alfred Tennyson, William Dean Howells, and Robert Louis Stevenson. Some of the periodicals were hiring photographers to cover a story so that an illustrator would have an accurate image from which to work. The *Daily Graphic* began to publish crudely reproduced photographs, but this practice was not being adapted by the others.

The public snatched up books of new fiction and of reissued classics with great relish as soon as they ap-peared. Often the works serialized in the monthlies ap-peared later in book form. Mark Twain's *Life on the Mississippi,* published in 1883, was well received particu-larly because it included material that had not been previously published. The critics condemned Robert Browning's new volume of poetry, which included "Aga-memnon," as being remarkably shallow.

Non-fiction was also receiving considerable attention. *Harper's Weekly* serialized William Graham Sumner's *What Social Classes Owe to Each Other.* Even before its publication in book form, the press had given great play to Sumner's pronouncement that the "aggregation of large fortunes . . . is a necessary condition of many forms of social advance. . . ."[15] Even in the realm of pop-ular history, young, multi-talented Theodore Roosevelt was gaining some notice for his new *The Naval War of 1812.*

Leisure Time

When the press covered amusements, its attention was almost always confined to the activities of the two cities' higher social strata. The pleasures of the poor received little coverage, and much of that was reserved for editorial instruction about the alleged evils of the dance hall and saloon.

The press and most of its readers were extraordinarily interested in the rituals of "society," and in the social Season which ran from the beginning of October until the end of June; the seasons in Newport, Saratoga Springs, and other resorts monopolized their attention for the remainder of the year.

The Good Life

Ticket to the Purim Celebration of the Young Men's Hebrew Association, at the Lexington Avenue Opera House, between 58th and 59th Streets. (Archives of the 92nd Street YM-YWHA)

The ball was society's most conspicuous activity. For the socially prominent, speculation about which elaborate event was going to be the ball of the year, not to mention what everyone invited would be wearing to it, kept one almost fully engrossed. In 1883, the Annual Charity Ball on January 25th at the Academy of Music was the first major ball of the new year, and every member of society was expected to attend. The lesser echelons of the upper classes had their own balls, many of which took place in Madison Square Garden. The Grand Carnival de l'Opera on January 18th drew a large and boisterous crowd. The Arion Ball, sponsored by the most socially prominent German association in New York, was held a month later. The Garden was lavishly decorated, and a sizable crowd turned out.

In both New York and Brooklyn, dancing classes and balls were held regularly for the Season's debutantes and

Invitation to the Arion Ball at Madison Square Garden. (Museum of the City of New York)

Mrs. Elliot F. Shepard, a daughter of William H. Vanderbilt, dressed as a marquise for the Vanderbilt Ball. (Museum of the City of New York)

young gentlemen. The ball given by Mrs. John Shults for her son John, Jr., was a typical affair: most of the attention was devoted, not to the young man, but to his sister, Alline, who, the press dutifully noted, wore white satin trimmed with point lace.

Undoubtedly, the ball of the 1883 Season—and the social event of the year—took place the day after Easter. This most lavish affair, a costume ball, was given by William K. Vanderbilt—or rather by his wife, Alva Smith Vanderbilt—at their Fifth Avenue home for a reported cost of $250,000, with $11,000 devoted entirely to the cost of flowers, and $4,000 to hairdressers. Mr. Vanderbilt was attired as the Duke de Guise, and Mrs. Vanderbilt portrayed a Venetian princess as painted by Cabanel. The other Vanderbilts were present, of course, each more elaborately dressed than the other; only William H. arrived in ordinary evening dress. Among the other 1,200 guests, Mr. and Mrs. Edward Leavitt came as a Bee and Hornet, and Miss Helen Buckley as Ice, with a gown of white tulle to which were attached many long glass icicles. Mrs. Burton N. Harrison, mother of the young diarist Reginald Fairfax Harrison, wore a blue satin dress of the First Empire with an overdress and train of gold gauze, a square-cut bodice with a gold spangled tulle fichu, and a gold lace ruff, all topped by an elaborate headdress. Mrs. Harrison's neighbor on Lexington Avenue, Abram Hewitt, came as King Lear—while still in his right mind, it was pointed out carefully. Wearing a costume of royal

Children of Five Points at play, photographed by Charles Smith. (Brooklyn Public Library, Brooklyn Collection)

85

purple velvet slashed with scarlet, the ubiquitous Ward McAllister portrayed a Huguenot, while Chauncey Depew appeared as an old Knickerbocker.

Next to the fashionable balls, weddings took up much of society's attention. Society weddings generally took place on Wednesdays. When Mrs. Lispenard Stewart's daughter, Mary Rhinelander Stewart, was married on Wednesday, April 25th, at Grace Church, it was a major social event of the season. And the marriage of Henry P. Morgan's daughter to Mr. J. Pendleton Schenck at St. Ann's in Brooklyn on Wednesday, October 21st, was another.

There were other weddings of the very rich that received far less attention in the press. When a Lehman was married in November, for example, all the prominent Jewish families were represented, but the ceremony itself was a quiet function that took place in the Lehman home. The weddings of rich Roman Catholics received even less notice than Jewish marriages.

When not busy with other duties, the gentleman of society had his club: the old Union Club, sometimes referred to as "the rich man's club"; the very Republican Union League Club; the Century Association, intended for the cultivation of art and literature, and limited to 100 members; the Harmony Club—*Gesellschaft Harmonie*—the club of the uptown Jews, which still conducted most of its affairs in German; and the University Club, which rented the Leonard Jerome mansion on Madison Square for its quarters.

Brooklyn's clubs—just as Brooklyn society—were more subdued. They included the New England Society, which promoted New England history and good fellowship among its members; the new Rembrandt Club, founded for the cultivation of the "gentler arts"; the Society of Old Brooklynites; the Pioneer Amateur Photographic Club; and a host of literary groups, such as the Bryant Literary Society.

Then there were the sporting clubs: the New York Athletic Club, which had just announced that it was about to build a new clubhouse on West 55th Street; the Coaching Club, whose purpose was to revive the pursuit of stagecoaching as a society sport; the American Jockey Club, which leased the Jerome Park race course in the Annexed District; and the New York Yacht Club on East 27th.

The new color called terra cotta seemed to be extremely popular, and many costumes were made of it, without any relief from any other tint. The result was that the ladies wearing them looked like a number of little earthen statuettes . . . and the effect was anything but pretty.

—Account of Mary Rhinelander Stewart's wedding

Brooklynites are quiet, home-loving, church-going, studious, and literary, rather than inclined to social gayety.

—*The Season*

May 26th, the annual parade of the Coaching Club. (*Harper's Weekly,* June 2, 1883; Brooklyn Public Library)

The club was almost always restricted to the white, Protestant male. Some of the older Sephardic families and the most elite of the German Jews had been accepted in several of them, such as the Union, the Union League, and the American Jockey Club. By the early eighties, however, some change could be detected. Since the late seventies, when the Grand Union Hotel in Saratoga had begun a policy of turning away Jews, the tensions that had resulted were spreading to Manhattan.

The women of society were generally kept absorbed by their many teas and charities. Several, Mrs. June Croly among them, believing that women should pursue interests of mutual benefit more actively, founded the Sorosis Club. Among its more ambitious goals was the co-education of women, particularly at Columbia College and NYU. Following the custom set by many of the men's clubs, Sorosis held its annual dinner at Delmonico's.

Some members of society had discovered that there was more to divert them than balls and weddings and clubs. Lectures and readings were often presented at Chickering Hall on Fifth Avenue and at private homes.

One could hear Matthew Arnold or Henry George, or spend an evening viewing a series of tableaux vivants based on Longfellow's poems. In March, Mrs. Burton N. Harrison held a gathering to honor a popular novelist, Frances Hodgson Burnett. Among the guests was the poet Emma Lazarus.

Their own amateur theater productions provided another diversion in which members of society immersed themselves. The Amaranth Amateur Dramatic Society, for example, performed at the Brooklyn Academy. The same Mrs. Harrison tried her hand at writing a drama, and her *A Russian Honeymoon* proved so popular that a professional production was mounted at the Madison Square Theatre.

Special projects also commanded considerable amounts of society's time. Raising funds to build the pedestal for the statue of Liberty was one. In New York and Brooklyn, committees formed to plan for soliciting contributions, benefits were held, and art "loan" exhibitions were organized.

When the press covered society events, it devoted considerable space to what society was wearing: indeed, society was preoccupied with its appearance as well. Women's spring and summer fashions for 1883 featured silks "in fine checks of all colors," dresses with "kilt pleated skirts of striped satin," and "black and white in combination."[16] While society women were still looking to Paris for the latest vogue, men were now leaning toward the English style. Ready-to-wear clothes were seen more and more, but signified a lack of class. The telltale crease in a pair of pants, for example, was simply unthinkable.

In '83, canvas shoes for men and women were all the rage. A.J. Cammeyer off Union Square advertised an enormous inventory of canvas shoes for lawn-tennis, bicycling, yachting, baseball, or seaside and mountain use. And H. Guilmard's near Cammeyer's promised that "the Langtry," a coiffure influenced by the English star, could be had by all.

In summer, society abandoned the city. By the first of July, the matrons of New York and Brooklyn would pack up their children and much of their households and set off for the seaside or the country. Often their husbands would stay in town until August, perhaps taking an occa-

The newest Parisian style to be worn at the seashore. (*Peterson's Magazine*, May 1883; author's collection)

The general tendency is toward mixed English suitings of plainer and neater fabrics than heretofore. . . . Trousers are cut medium tight, without spring, but the general tendency is to be but a trifle larger than heretofore.

—The *Brooklyn Advance*

sional evening excursion to Brighton Beach and visiting the family retreat on weekends.

Newport was the summer watering place of the elite. The presence of the prominent figures of society—Vanderbilt, Lorrillard, Livingston, Low, Belmont, and a few lords and ladies—ensured that this was so. Residing in their sumptuous "cottages" or in lavish hotels, they would repeat much the same routine as they had in New York. As a solid member of Brooklyn society, Henry E. Pierrepont was astonished that, after having spent such a strenuous social season during the winter, New Yorkers did not find Newport life just "too fatiguing to be continued all Summer."[17]

In mid-August, society's attention swiftly turned to Saratoga Springs, where many of the same people who had summered in Newport, plus some new ones—such as Mayor Edson and the Brooklyn civic leader James S.T. Stranahan—were in evidence. Some were there to take the waters, and some to view the races, but all were there to be seen.

While the wealthier and newer society was enjoying Newport and Saratoga, or spending the summer in Europe, the older New York and Brooklyn families sought the quiet country life. In August 1883, Reverend Wells of Williamsburgh left for Pine Hill in the Catskills, staying at the Crystal Spring Cottage and preaching at nearby communities. Late in the month he fell ill and traveled to Saratoga, where he took the waters. Henry Pierrepont, who had left at the end of June with his wife and fourteen pieces of luggage for Lake Lucerne near Lake George, also visited Saratoga, where he encountered, among others, the Stranahans at the United States Hotel. Henry Ward Beecher, who usually went to the country, planned a trip across the continent to visit a son in Oregon and hoped to return on the Northern Pacific Railroad, in which he had some interest.

Come September, the vacationers would be packed back into the city, ostensibly refreshed and eager to settle themselves back into the affairs they had fled in June. The ladies of society would be seen strolling on Broadway and Fifth Avenue, anxious to order the new fall fashions and to display their slightly bronzed complexions. There would be the usual teas to plan the balls and dinners, and then, all at once, the fall Season would begin.

Other than several free reading rooms, two museums, the public baths in summer, religious and ethnic festivals, and special events organized by charity groups, there was little public amusement to be enjoyed by those of modest circumstances or less, and certainly little that the press cared to note. Journalists insistently lectured the affluent for depriving the lower classes of recreational activity, particularly for decreeing that museums and libraries be closed on Sundays, pointing out that while everything else was shut, the saloons and other unsavory establishments were very much open.

A great many houses of entertainment which featured musical and comic spectacles were quite respectable and drew a large sector of the populace. Only elite society labeled them immoral. They included: Tony Pastor's Theatre, which opened to immediate success in 1881 in Tammany Hall on East 14th; the Thalia Theatre, the former Bowery Theatre, now devoted to German entertainment; the Atlantic Garden, nearby; Koster and Bial's Concert Hall on West 23rd, which featured a vaudeville hall and beer garden; Niblo's Theatre in the Metropolitan Hotel; and the popular Harlem Garden, uptown. Panoramas

Public Amusement

The February 19, 1883 program for Tony Pastor's Theatre. (New York Public Library at the Lincoln Center for the Performing Arts, Billy Rose Theatre Collection)

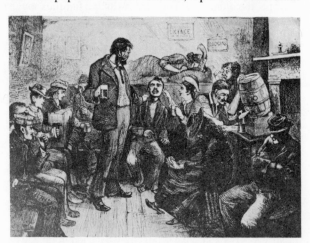

The wicked and disreputable saloon, this one in Five Points. (*Harper's Weekly,* February 28, 1880; Brooklyn Public Library)

were also in style. The Belgian Panorama on West 57th featured the "Seige of Paris," lighted by electricity for the first time in 1883.

The more tawdry establishments received the bulk of a curious and outraged public's condemnation. Most prominent among these was Harry Hill's on Houston, a bawdy saloon and dance hall not far from police headquarters. It was often noted by genteel observers that if the police didn't know what went on in Harry Hill's, they were the only ones who didn't. The main attraction was the boxing match.

Those engaged in moral uplift fought hard against Harry Hill's, the Sultan Divan, and other haunts they deemed to be degenerate. They gathered and displayed statistics—10,000 liquor stores in New York, one to every 125 residents; 2,300 neighborhood taverns in Brooklyn for example—to arouse the fears of the refined and the well-bred, or those who aspired to be. Anthony Comstock's Society for the Suppression of Vice was only one of the groups that attempted to rally the populace around its cause. And almost all of the old set of New York society, and all of Brooklyn's, were active in temperance work. Reverend Wells, for one, was a zealous worker in the effort to minimize the number of liquor licenses which the Brooklyn Board of Excise could grant to saloon keepers.

Culture

The middle and upper strata of the two cities' populations could enjoy a vast assortment of art, music, and drama. Yet, as was so often the case in other realms, Brooklynites had to suffer being measured against New York, and New Yorkers had to suffer parallel comparisons with Europe.

The art world offered a perfect example. In 1880, the

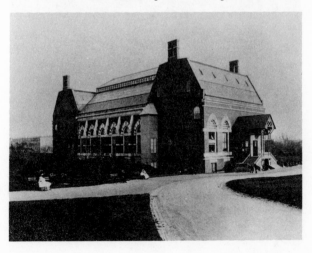

The new building of the Metropolitan Museum in Central Park; its rear faces Fifth Avenue and 82nd Street. (Museum of the City of New York)

Metropolitan Museum moved into its own building on Fifth Avenue. Because of its location in Central Park, it had agreed to open free of charge on certain days; it charged twenty-five cents on the others. Attendance by those who were not members of society, however, was rare. While praised for its attempts to create a true art museum in less than fifteen years, the Museum was being chastised nevertheless for not actually having accomplished it.

The other major art institution in Manhattan, the National Academy of Design, quartered in an ornate Venetian palace on East 23rd, drew a great deal of attention during its spring and autumn exhibitions, but these were treated more as social events than as serious displays of art. The work of Thomas Eakins was quite popular, and John Singer Sargent was getting some notice, although the critics wondered whether he would ever achieve great stature. The Brooklyn Art Association on Montague Street also held spring and fall exhibitions, but they could hardly be expected to compare with the Academy's. The commercial art galleries, such as Goupil's, were said to be far inferior to those in Europe.

The chief characteristic of this year's exhibition at the National Academy was, I think, its commonplaceness. It was extremely level, and its level was one of discouraging mediocrity.

—Review by Maria Griswold van Rensselaer

The Spring Exhibition at the National Academy of Design. (*Harper's Weekly,* April 29, 1882; Brooklyn Public Library)

Like the Metropolitan, the American Museum of Natural History, situated on West 77th in Manhattan Square, was open free of charge at certain times of the week. Because of its location on the underpopulated west side, attendance was low, and one could easily question

The north side of East 14th Street, with Tony Pastor's in Tammany Hall on the left, and the Academy of Music, with canopy, next door. (Museum of the City of New York)

Most of her efforts were attended with applause so earnest and long continued that her performance was brought to a standstill.

—Review of Adelina Patti in *Il Trovatore*

whether the ambitious plans to construct an extensive complex would ever come to fruition.

The Academy of Music was New York's major music hall. It was here that the Philharmonic played and where New York's opera season, perhaps without equal, was centered. Patti and Modjeska performed here, although they were sometimes forced to tolerate frightful productions. But the Academy, firmly established on East 14th Street for thirty years, was now threatened. A number of the new rich, apparently offended by the Academy's exclusive subscription policies, organized to subscribe for a new hall. In October 1883, their uptown creation, the Metropolitan Opera House, was to open. Other concert halls were also extremely popular. Both Steinway Hall on East 14th and Chickering Hall, farther north on Fifth Avenue, were associated with piano manufacturers; their concerts helped to promote their products. Brooklyn's gigantic brick and stone Academy of Music, also designed by Leopold Eidlitz, served Brooklyn's purpose ideally. All the great musicians and singers performed there, just as they performed in other major cities like St. Louis and Chicago.

On occasion, an event was held not simply to financially benefit the less fortunate, but to entertain them. In March of '83, William Rhinelander Stewart began organizing a series of band concerts to be given in Washington Square especially for the poorer residents of the area.

With subscriptions collected from among his society friends, the concerts were to run from May until the funds ran out. They were a great success, and as the *Tribune* noted, well attended, particularly by "children of every size, condition and color," who came to hear the Seventh Regiment Band play Gilbert and Sullivan selections, Strauss waltzes, and Harrigan and Hart melodies.[18]

One area in which the citizens of New York did not have to feel inferior to their European brethren was the theatre. And next to Manhattan, Brooklyn probably supported more theatres per capita than any other American city. The most prominent were the Park and Standard on Fulton Street, Haverly's Brooklyn Theatre and Hyde & Behman's nearby, with two in the Eastern District, the Broadway and the Williamsburgh Lyceum. The *New York Mirror*, the major theatre tabloid, warned that the Brooklyn Bridge would make it easier for Brooklynites to travel to Manhattan's theatre district, and that Brooklyn entrepreneurs would have to produce more original and innovative work.

New York had so many theatres—someone counted over 40,000 seats—that one had to wonder how they could all realize good profits. But as old ones went out of business, new ones were always taking their places. Most of them were clustered around Madison Square and to the north, but a few remained downtown. The old Wallack's below Union Square reopened as the Star in March. Oscar Wilde opened his new play, *Vera*, at the Union Square Theatre at the end of August; it was given very little notice.

The Park Theatre just below Madison Square burned in October 1882, the day Lillie Langtry was to have made her debut there. Rumor had it that Brooks Brothers would build on the site; Hyde & Behman of Brooklyn were building a new Park Theatre farther uptown. Mrs. Langtry made her long-awaited debut in early November at the brand new Palmer's Theatre at 30th Street; she returned in '83, appearing as Galatea at the nearby Fifth Avenue Theatre.

Booth's Theatre near Madison Square was scheduled to close in mid-1883. One of its last offerings, *Monte Cristo*, had a big cast headed by James O'Neill and an elaborate production, but, as the *Mirror* put it, "the fine scenery seemed . . . to emphasize the very mediocre acting."[19] Mrs. Harrison's successful romantic comedy, *A*

Her performance . . . justified . . . the opinion that with constant training, she may in time become a competent actress. . . .

—Review of Lillie Langtry in
Pygmalion and Galatea

The first on-stage photograph of a play, *A Russian Honeymoon*, taken with the use of specially installed Brush electric lights; Agnes Booth is standing at the spinning wheel, and producer Daniel Frohman, who donned a uniform, is the tall man in the center. (Museum of the City of New York)

Russian Honeymoon, starring Agnes Booth, opened in April at the three-year-old Madison Square Theatre.

Perhaps as a portent of the future, the Moorish-style Casino Theatre had opened in late 1882 on Broadway at 39th Street, opposite the new opera house. And when in mid-December 1883, the Standard, just south of 32nd, —so fondly remembered for the American debut of Gilbert and Sullivan's *H.M.S. Pinafore*—was hit by fire, a decision was made to rebuild on the same site.

The 1883 theatre season promised to be remarkable. Appearances by Joseph Jefferson, Ada Rehan and John Drew, James O'Neill, Lillie Langtry, Ellen Terry, and Henry Irving were just some of the highlights. At the Star, Irving's American debut performance in *The Bells* overwhelmed the critics, one of whom called it "thrilling in its intensity," and "at moments inspiring to awe."[20]

In a lighter vein, Harrigan and Hart were reviving some of their older musical comedies, including the great favorite, *The Mulligan Guard Ball*. And 1883 would be Jumbo's second year in P.T. Barnum's circus.

Sports

Recreation in the two cities, like so much else, revolved primarily around the tastes of society. In the early eighties, the two cities—if not the entire country—witnessed an enormous revival in both competitive and spectator sports.

Lawn tennis had become an immensely popular pursuit for men and women in the last few years. More than 125 separate tennis clubs were formed in Brooklyn and organized to play in Prospect Park. At times, the Parks Department marked out as many as eighty courts on the park's Long Meadow—a circumstance which, of course, greatly exasperated the park's self-appointed protectors.

In winter, skating was a favorite diversion. As soon as the ponds at the edges of each city froze, flocks of skaters would take to the ice. And whenever the red ball was raised at the lake at Central Park to indicate that the ice was safe, so many turned out that there was scarcely room to move. After a good snowfall, sleighing parties would be out in full regalia, and Central Park and the avenues north became "a scene of flying horses, dashing sleighs, cracking whips, and gay drivers."[21]

In the warmer months, the opportunities for amusement seemed endless. Picnicking and strolling were com-

Tennis on the Long Meadow in Prospect Park. (The Long Island Historical Society)

A bench in Union Square. (New York Public Library Picture Collection)

mon pastimes that all could enjoy. The picnic would often be the culmination of a boat excursion up the Hudson or East rivers, or out to Bath or Coney Island. The working classes often participated in organized outings at Jones's Wood on the East River, or to Pope's Park in South Brooklyn. The heat of the summer brought the cities' residents out for an evening stroll. Those who had the leisure enjoyed ambling down Broadway after dark to take in the new electric lamps.

Sunday drives were most in fashion among the wealthy, who could parade their horses and carriages out Ocean Parkway to Coney Island, or through Central Park, up one of Harlem's avenues, and across the Harlem River to the Annexed District. There, the merry riding parties would often end up at one of the road houses—perhaps Gabe Case's, Judge Smith's, or Florence's.

Decoration Day announced the beginning of the racing season at Jerome Park in the Annexed District. Two packed trains arrived from Grand Central Depot for the events of the afternoon. The bluff below the clubhouse was filled with the coaches of the fashionable set, who were enjoying their picnic lunches nearby. And at Leonard Jerome's Sheepshead Bay race course, a younger equally fashionable crowd turned out for Derby Day in June.

Another group of New York society members organized the National Horse Show Association, and staged its first exhibition in late October at Madison Square Garden. With the arena filled to capacity for every event, the Association was encouraged to think that the show might become an annual occurrence. Yachting was yet another

Masthead of the music program for the Brighton Beach Hotel. (The Long Island Historical Society)

fascination of society. Races took place almost every week on Long Island Sound and New York Bay. The annual regatta of the New York Yacht Club in June brought out more than 5,000 spectators to the Bay.

By July 4th, the Coney Island resorts were in full swing. For those of comfortable means who did not leave town for the length of the summer, the hotels and restaurants there provided a fine respite. By mid-August the place was jammed, and stayed that way until the end of September, when everything shut down.

Breading Way's photograph of the beach at Coney Island. (Brooklyn Public Library, Brooklyn Collection)

One could reach Coney Island from Brooklyn on any of nine steam railways and one horse-car line, and from Manhattan by steam boat and then rail. A single entrepreneur often owned the transportation line that terminated at his hotel and special extravaganza. When the Long Island Railroad announced its reduced summer rates to Coney Island, it was seeking not only new riders, but also customers for its Oriental and Manhattan Beach hotels. In '83, the Iron Steam-Boat Company inaugurated its cool, clean, quick, and safe all-water route from the end of the Battery to Coney Island, with the bonus of a live spectacle at the point of destination. Each promoter attempted to outdo the other, whether it was with the "Bombardment of Alexandria," "Gilmore's World Renowned Band," or the new

"Buffalo Bill and Dr. Carver's Wild West Exhibition."

The most ornate of the Coney Island hotels was the Manhattan Beach, whose guests were drawn from the better classes of New York. The hotel was almost 700 feet long, with dining facilities that could serve 4,000 at a single sitting. The *carte du jour* for one mid-July day included among its entrees "Soft Shell Crabs in cases a l'Oriental," and "Croquettes of English Snipe, Chasseur," twenty fish and shellfish dishes, twenty-six kinds of steak, and an assortment of other dishes, from "Calf's Head a la vinaigrette," to "Omelette a la Espagnole," several dozen vegetables, including twelve styles of potatoes, over fifty desserts and cheeses, and an immense selection of champagnes, clarets, wines, madeiras, sherries, brandies, whiskies, lagers, ales, porters, mineral waters, and cordials.[22] Because it was more of a family resort, the only slightly less elegant Brighton Beach Hotel catered to the Brooklyn set.

Some were saying in '83 that the entire resort was becoming a little run down. Three-Card Monte swindlers created a real problem on the beach, duping the innocent and annoying almost everyone else. But with some five million visitors a year, Coney Island was hardly in trouble.

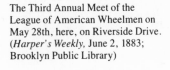

The Third Annual Meet of the League of American Wheelmen on May 28th, here, on Riverside Drive. (*Harper's Weekly,* June 2, 1883; Brooklyn Public Library)

Of all the leisure-time activities, two—bicycling and baseball—were causing near-pandemonium. So many people were riding bicycles, and so many accidents were occurring, that the Park Commissioners of both cities were stymied about how to arrive at a peaceful solution.

After some deliberation, the Brooklyn Commissioners decreed that Brooklyn bicycle riders were sufficiently expert to use Prospect Park. But in Manhattan, the Commissioners banned riding altogether in Central Park. After one complaint reached the State Supreme Court, the Commissioners relented, opening the park to experienced riders with permits, but only on the West Drive between sunrise and 9 a.m.

Many bicycling clubs formed, including the Kings County Wheelmen, which sponsored races at the Williamsburgh Athletic Club grounds. The major club was the League of American Wheelmen. On May 28th, Reginald Fairfax Harrison was among thousands who went to watch the parade of 750 riders at its Third Annual Meet wind through Central Park and onto Riverside Drive.

Baseball had recently overtaken cricket as the country's primary spectator sport. Almost everyone enjoyed baseball, whether amateur, semi-professional, or big-league. A sad announcement of 1883 was that one of the game's most popular spots, the Union Grounds in the Eastern District, would be redeveloped for housing and

The Mets, drawn from a photograph by Sarony; standing fourth from the left is Edward Kennedy, left field. (*Harper's Weekly,* August 5, 1882; Brooklyn Public Library)

After lunch I went . . . up to the Polo grounds to see the match between the Mets & Athletics. After some very poor playing on the Mets part, except Kennedy . . . they were licked badly (11 to 4). . . . It was very hot today.

—Reginald Fairfax Harrison

commercial uses, and soon the "cheers that once shook the grand stand" would be mere memories.[23]

New York's big-league teams were the Metropolitans in the American Association and the New York Base-ball Club in the National Base-ball League. The 1883 National League Championship was won by the Boston Club, with New York coming in sixth. In the American Association, Philadelphia came in first, and the New York Mets were fourth, although by the end of the season their record had improved considerably. The Brooklyn Club, which was playing at the new Washington Grounds at Fourth Avenue and 3rd Street near the Gowanus Canal, was in the Inter-State Association. The club won the association's championship in '83.

The Year at a Glance

January

As soon as the holiday season had come and gone, and New Year's had passed, the year 1883 began full speed ahead. Franklin Edson assumed office as mayor, and, in his first address, recounted the great accomplishments of the City of New York but contended that much was left to be achieved in regard to the delivery of services. The press received the Mayor's speech with its typical reserve.

January was a month of charity balls, soirees, and cold weather. On January 23rd the Nineteenth Century Club met at the home of Mrs. Courtlandt Palmer on East 21st Street to hear Julia Ward Howe reminisce about the two recently departed New Englanders, Emerson and Longfellow.

February

Saturday, February 3rd, was the occasion of one of the year's major social events: the Bartholdi Statue Fund Benefit at the New York Academy of Music. It was called a "brilliant social gathering" by the *Times*, and the guests pretty much were oblivious of the fact that they were attending a performance of a farce, *Was He Right*, and that their presence was helping to pay for the statue of Liberty's pedestal.[24] On February 14th, the cities' populations read that Richard Wagner had died rather suddenly in Venice.

March

March 17th was St. Patrick's day, as usual, but this year's parade from the Cooper Union up to Jones's Wood was the smallest in several years. Mayor Edson turned out at the Friendly Sons of St. Patrick's dinner at Delmonico's, just as Mayor Low attended the St. Patrick's Society of Brooklyn dinner at Mansion House. On the same day, the papers affirmed the death of Karl Marx. The next day, reports began to appear regarding a telephone call made successfully over a long distance, some 701 miles from New York to Cleveland, Ohio. On March 21st, Jumbo and the rest of Barnum's circus came to town, marching from Morrisania in the Annexed District, across the Harlem River, down Fifth Avenue, and then over to Madison Square Garden, where they were scheduled to open with great revelry on the 26th. Easter Sunday 1883 fell on March 25th. Although the holiday was not considered a particularly important one, churchgoers always took pleasure in displaying their finery along Fifth Avenue.

The ball—and thus the event—of the Season took place the next evening. Such an elaborate spectacle as the

Vanderbilt Ball had never taken place in New York before, and one could only imagine what it would lead to in the future. The papers gossiped about the ball for weeks ahead of time, and did not stop for weeks afterward.

April

Portrait of Peter Cooper who died on April 4th. (*Harper's Weekly,* April 14, 1883; Brooklyn Public Library)

Chief Engineer Washington A. Roebling. (Rutgers University Library, Special Collections Department, Roebling Papers)

This was the month the fashionable shops had their spring openings. The new Fulton Market was scheduled to open on the 2nd, but so few stands were ready that the official opening was postponed until the 4th. On Wednesday, April 4th, the long beloved Peter Cooper died at the Hewitt home on Lexington Avenue. The funeral on April 7th took place at All Souls' Unitarian Church nearby, and flags were flown throughout the city at half-mast. New York seemed to stop moving for that moment. The pallbearers included Hamilton Fish, A.A. Low, the publisher William Appleton, and Cyrus Field. The funeral was followed by a procession down to the ferry and out to Green-Wood Cemetery. Within a few days, many proposals for a fitting monument were announced, including one for a memorial that would stand in the tiny park at the juncture of Third and Fourth Avenues just below the Cooper Union, although there was some immediate reaction that the site was not appropriate.

There was much excitement about the phenomenon of the almost-completed Brooklyn Bridge. The press was both extolling and ridiculing its existence, but no one could ignore its imminent opening. A group of ruffians managed to get onto the bridge, creating a ruckus and causing the police to waste many hours in pursuit before they could be removed. Some residents of Brooklyn feared that unless the bridge trustees decided to charge a toll for pedestrians, the "scum of New York" would invade their city.[25] Asked to respond, Mayor Low declared that such people were too lazy to walk across the bridge even if it were free. Other residents feared that they, as Brooklyn taxpayers, would be saddled with the burden of paying for its maintenance unless some fee was charged to users. Shop owners on Fulton Street worried that if a proposal to extend Flatbush Avenue to the bridge were to become a reality, Fulton would end up as a back street with little trade.

By late April, plans were afoot for the bridge's opening ceremonies on May 24th. The Brooklyn Sunday School Association, which always held its anniversary parade on the 24th, was dismayed, and suggested that the opening date be moved. Others felt even more slighted. The 24th was Queen Victoria's birthday, and visiting British dignitaries were expected at the ceremonies honoring their Queen on that day. And that the bridge was to open on the British Queen's birthday seemed a bitter slur to the many Irish workers who had labored on completing it.

The next to last week in April, the circus came to the Hippodrome on Fulton Avenue in Brooklyn. P. T. Barnum advertised that his "greatest show on earth" would include "Eight monster nightly shows. . . . Enormous museum of living curiosities," and "Comical, humorous, laughable, amusing, difficult and puzzling obstacle races."[26]

Following a long tradition, the first day of May in New York and Brooklyn was moving day. Carts, wagons, vans, and every other conceivable sort of conveyance could be seen moving through all parts of each city and back and forth on the ferries. Although a new tenant might still get the first month's rent free, the costs of moving had risen alarmingly, so that there was less inducement to change one's residence. On May 6th, the ship *Alaska* arrived at Sandy Hook from England in the record time of six days, twenty-three hours and forty-eight minutes. On the 14th, "ten thousand men shrieked themselves hoarse . . . over the greatest glove contest ever fought in New York."[27] Both the rich and the not-so-rich watched John L. Sullivan outmaneuver Charley Mitchell in three rounds at the bout at Madison Square Garden. On May 12th, Mrs. Burton Harrison held one of the frequent meetings that took place at her home, this one to organize subcommittees for an Art Loan Exhibition for the statue of Liberty pedestal.

By the second week in May, the papers began to fill with articles about the bridge: its history, the story of its designer, John Roebling, his tragic death, the work of his successor, his son, Washington A. Roebling, and that of Washington's wife, Emily, Washington's alleged incapacitation as a result of the caisson disease, his refusal to relinquish his post as Chief Engineer in spite of his long absence, the financial and political scandals that plagued the bridge's progress, the many long years of toil and loss of life, the cable railway which was still unfinished, the various tolls to be charged vehicles and pedestrians, and, at last, its completion. Already, there was talk about the

It is a noble work—We expected to feel dizzy at its elevation, but it is so broad & solid. . . . It took 20 minutes to cross & I preferred to return to Brooklyn in our comfortable ferryboat.

—Henry E. Pierrepont,
   March 19, 1883

May

We went to the Brooklyn Bridge and walked over and back again and threw stones at the boats underneath and Havemeyer hit a man on the ferry.

—Reginald Fairfax Harrison,
   May 12, 1883

UNITED!

Brooklyn and New York by the Great Bridge.

THE MIGHTY STRUCTURE COMPLETED

Page One headlines of the *Brooklyn Eagle,* May 24th. (The Long Island Historical Society)

After my Latin I got excused and went down to City Hall on the "L" road and then went to the opening of the Bridge and showed my ticket . . . I thought I would never get over but I did at last. . . . Then Mr. J. Levy played a cornet solo which was the best thing done and he was applauded so much that he wanted to keep it up but Mr. Hewitt wanted to make his oration and so he commenced but the solo played on and nobody paid any attention to Mr. Hewitt. At last the cornet stopped and Mr Hewitt commenced to talk . . . but it was so deep that I left. . . . I went over to papa's office and . . . he told me I could go on the roof of the Equitable Building tonight. . . . We saw most of the fireworks. They weren't half what I thought they would be but it was fun. . . . Today was a splendid day.

—Reginald Fairfax Harrision,
  May 24, 1883

need for a second bridge, even a tunnel. One of the special and privileged treats was to secure a pass to cross the bridge before it officially opened. In Brooklyn, Henry Pierrepont and his neighbors were kept busy making preparations for decorating their houses and streets for the opening celebration. The Annual Sunday School Parade —defying tradition—was held on May 23rd. The children sang their songs and marched along the various appointed routes just as had been done for so many years.

Beginning at about 12:40 p.m. on Thursday, the 24th, a contingent of mounted police and the Seventh Regiment met President Arthur, Governor Cleveland, and other dignitaries at the Fifth Avenue Hotel and escorted them down Fifth Avenue. The streets were crowded with spectators of all ages. Many Brooklyn businesses were closed for the day, and many New York businesses closed for the afternoon; Brooklyn schools were closed for the day and many in New York closed for the afternoon. At City Hall, the procession met Mayor Edson and then made its way to the bridge's New York tower, where it was joined by the bridge trustees. The parade proceeded across the bridge, with appropriate fanfare of bands, ships, cannon, and church bells, to the Brooklyn tower, where Mayor Low and Mrs. Emily Roebling were waiting, and the entire assemblage made its way to the Brooklyn terminus for the formal ceremonies. After much music and many lengthy and optimistic speeches, the ceremonies ended. The dignitaries then proceeded to the Roebling home on Columbia Heights for a reception, and later, dinner at the Mayor's.

As dark came, the seventy Weston electric arc lamps were turned on. At 8:00 a large and long display of fireworks was set off from the bridge, viewed by all those who could find space on nearby roofs. At the end of the evening, a reception was given in honor of the President and the Governor at the Brooklyn Academy of Music.

The opening ceremonies came and went. Again, the dailies and weeklies were full of the story of the great enterprise. Residents of the two cities rushed to cross the river over their new bridge, but as far as the press was concerned, by the 26th the story was over.

Attention turned to international matters. Alexander III was crowned Czar of all Russia, amidst stories of anti-Jewish activity. A treaty between Corea and the United States was ratified, marking the first the Asian kingdom

had concluded with an outside power. Decoration Day, May 30th, was cool, not a good day for the shore. An unusually large number of people remained in town. President Arthur viewed the annual parade down Broadway from a grandstand in Madison Square. In Brooklyn the various divisions of that city's parade broke off and continued on to the various cemeteries. Thousands of both cities' residents took the opportunity of the holiday to cross the new bridge, so many that a panic occurred; twelve were crushed to death, and many more were injured. The press devoted more space to the panic than it had to the opening. Editorials instructed that the disaster could have been prevented, and, in fact, that nothing approaching it need ever occur again.

The fireworks on the evening of May 24th. (*Frank Leslie's Illustrated Newspaper,* June 2, 1883; Rutgers University Library, Special Collections Department, Roebling Papers)

June

The weather grew warmer, and the school year came to a close. The graduating class of the Brooklyn Collegiate and Polytechnic Institute held its commencement at the Academy of Music and, at the end of the formalities, marched from Montague Street across the Brooklyn Bridge and back before parting.

July

The papers of July 3rd reported that General George Crook had stopped off in Denver on his way to Washington to report that, contrary to rumor, Indian hostilities had come to an end. On the 3rd, the cities suffered from a terrible wind and rain storm, after which a heat spell set in.

July 4th, which fell on a Wednesday, was very hot, a sizzling 95 degrees. The day was fairly quiet, and almost everything was closed. There were the normal artillery salutes, cannon fire, flag-raisings, parades, boat excursions, picnics, and fireworks.

After many protestations over the wild driving on the bridge, the trustees announced at their July 9th meeting that the speed limit would be set at four miles an hour. The press quickly figured out that at that rate it would take a vehicle at least twenty minutes to cross, a fact that should have delighted the ferry owners. The trustees also confirmed the appointment of no less than seventy-five police for duty on the bridge, a concession which still did not quiet the complaints that alarmingly few men were patrolling it. At the same time, the trustees received the resignation of Washington A. Roebling as the bridge's Chief Engineer.

"General Tom Thumb," the former star of Barnum's circus, died on the 15th in his home in Massachusetts. On July 30th, "Buffalo Bill and Dr. Carver's Wild West Exhibition" opened at the Prospect Park Fairgrounds in Gravesend, featuring 136 Indians, cowboys, and Mexicans, and 100 horses, wild buffalos, elk, deer, and Texas steer.

August

The two cities were very quiet. Most of the news came from out of town. President Arthur opened the still unfinished Southern Exposition in Louisville, Kentucky, on August 1st. Late in the month, Henry Villard escorted a large party of invited dignitaries and colleagues by Pullman car to Helena in Montana Territory for the opening ceremonies of his Northern Pacific Railroad. The long ride West seemed to confirm the fears of many of its investors—that the railroad simply went nowhere. Toward the end of the month, reports were received from Panama that Ferdinand de Lesseps' work on the canal was progressing well, and that the enterprise should be completed within five years.

On August 28th, the boiler of the steamer *Riverdale* burst on the Hudson just south of 23rd Street, killing five and injuring fifteen. Jay Gould, who was on his way out to his steamer, the *Atlantic*, signalled his crew to go to the distressed ship's aid. Also on the 28th, the papers gave some small mention of reports of some explosions in the Pacific. It was not until at least a week later that the first horror stories of the fatal volcanic eruptions of Krakatoa appeared.

The second annual picnic of the Central Labor Union was held on Wednesday, September 5th at Elm Park in upper Manhattan, preceded by a parade of more than 6,000 union men which passed the reviewing stands in Union Square. After completing the lavish trip West, Villard's party was among the some 3,000 who witnessed the driving of the last spike of the Northern Pacific on September

September

The Central Labor Union's annual parade, passing by the reviewing stand at Union Square. (*Frank Leslie's Illustrated Newspaper,* September 16, 1882; Brooklyn Public Library)

8th at Gold Creek, thirty miles west of Helena.

In mid-September, the first regularly scheduled cable car run took place, but not without much whining that the cars were too crowded, and that one was required to change to still another conveyance at the other end, a situation that was considered to be ridiculous. Public and private schools opened for the year, and the finer shops of the two cities were holding their fall openings to unveil the latest finery. The Season had begun.

October

On October 1st, domestic postage was reduced from three to two cents. The Jewish New Year, the year 5644, began at sunset on the same day. On October 7th, Mayor Edson officially opened the annual American Institute Fair on East 63rd Street. The exhibition was filled with displays of the latest in the domestic arts, commerce, and industry. (When the fair closed in December, some 70,000 had viewed steam-ship models, an elevator, gas stoves, and a pyramid of biscuits and wafers, and sampled all the popular products, including Boston baked beans.)

With the exception of the Vanderbilt Ball, the opening of the Metropolitan Opera House on October 22nd was the event of the Season. That morning, the cities experienced an early snow, but only a few flakes fell. J.C. Cady, the designer of the extraordinarily elaborate yellow brick Italian Renaissance-style building, particularly prided himself on having created a structure that was fireproof. The stage was the largest in the city. Opening night was long awaited, and both old and new money vied for the best boxes. The first performance was of Gounod's *Faust*, sung by two of opera's most celebrated stars, Italo Campanini and Christine Nilsson, but the glitter of the occasion itself far overshadowed the evening's performances.

When the opening notes of the overture sounded through the house there was a momentary hush, and then as if everybody had made his bow and done his duty by that everybody turned to his neighbor and began to chat in the liveliest manner. . . . But when the curtain arose the conversation ceased at once.

—The *Tribune*, describing the opening of the Metropolitan Opera

109

The Broadway elevation of the Metropolitan Opera House. (*Harper's New Monthly Magazine*, November 1883; Brooklyn Public Library)

In late October, Matthew Arnold, the English poet and essayist, arrived in the United States and gave his first lecture at Chickering Hall. The press noted that Halloween festivities on the 31st seemed limited almost entirely to the tossing of flour by rowdy young boys at innocent passersby.

November

At the beginning of November, the Louisville Exposition closed. It was declared to have been a great success; some 800,000 had visited its manufacturing and agricultural exhibits. One of the most popular features had been the Edison lamps, which had been turned on every evening. On November 13th, elaborate ceremonies were held at the New York Academy of Music to honor the 400th anniversary of Martin Luther's birth, including musical selections by the Oratorio Society conducted by Leopold Damrosch, and a speech by the noted Boston minister, Reverend Phillips Brooks.

At 12:00 noon on Sunday, November 18th, time in the two cities was suspended for nearly four minutes. The railroad companies were adopting Standard Time, compressing some seventy-five different standards for keeping time across the continent into four zones: Eastern, Central, Rocky Mountain, and Pacific. Some feared that disaster was sure to occur, but in the end, time began again, and all went on as usual. Two days later, the Second Annual Hebrew Ball took place at the Brooklyn Academy of Music, to benefit the Hebrew Orphan Asylum.

Then the flotilla passed up into the mist, whence it presently emerged, and steaming out into the Bay the vessels vanished one after another, and became spectral ships in the fog.

—Description of the parade of ships on Evacuation Day

The following Sunday, November 25th, was the one hundredth anniversary of the evacuation of the British from New York at the end of the American Revolution. The event was commemorated the following day. On probably the gloomiest, rawest, windiest, and rainiest Monday of the year, thousands poured into the streets to celebrate Evacuation Day, and hail once more the proud veterans of the past wars. Although no legal holiday had been declared, very little business transpired. The city was festooned with flags and streamers, and the morning

The unveiling of the statue of George Washington on the steps of the Sub-treasury, November 26th. (Museum of the City of New York)

festivities included loud reports of cannon fire, a parade down Broadway, and a procession of nearly 300 ships through the harbor. Then, at 1:23 p.m., according to the Trinity Church clock, Governor Cleveland released a silk cord to reveal the long-awaited statue of George Washington that had been installed on the steps of the Sub-treasury on Wall Street, at the very site of his inauguration as the nation's first President. That evening, the Chamber of

111

Commerce, which had commissioned the sculptor J.Q.A. Ward to create the statue, gave a dinner at Delmonico's for President Arthur and other dignitaries. An even more exclusive affair was held at the Hotel Brunswick for eighty-three descendants of the nation's oldest families. The next day, the morning papers announced that black lecturer and advocate for women's rights Sojourner Truth had died the day before at the age of 108.

Friday, November 30th, was Thanksgiving. Those who could afford it enjoyed the traditional dinner of turkey, cranberry, fruits and vegetables, and pumpkin or mince pie.

December

On December 3rd, the Art Loan Exhibition for the Bartholdi Fund opened at the Academy of Design. The collection included paintings, lace, and jewels. At the opening, a poem written for the collection by Emma Lazarus was read aloud. Its title was "The New Colossus."

Mrs. Henry Villard gave a tea at her Fifth Avenue residence on Sunday, December 16th. On Monday, Mr. Villard moved his family to its new home at Madison and 50th. On Tuesday, Villard failed to appear at his office in the Mills Building, amid speculations that investors were pulling out of the Northern Pacific. Villard claimed that he was merely engaged in the details of settling his family in its new quarters.

Friday, December 21st, was the Fourth Annual Festival of the New England Society of Brooklyn, held to honor the Pilgrim fathers. The guests, including President Chester A. Arthur, General Ulysses S. Grant, Mayor Seth Low, Henry E. Pierrepont, and Reverend Henry Ward Beecher, dined well on oysters, shrimp or beef soup, sea bass and sheepshead a la Chambord, filet of beef, stuffed capon, terrapin Newburg, canvas-back duck, quail, and a large assortment of liquors and desserts. On Christmas, sledding and sleighing parties were out enjoying over a foot of freshly fallen snow. There was considerable relief that the traditional messy Christmas tree was losing favor to the Christmas stocking.

By the end of the month, excavations began on Bedloe's Island to erect the base for the statue of Liberty, but the combination of cold weather and lack of money was slowing everything down. Richard Morris Hunt had received the commission to design the pedestal, but some-

Portrait of Emma Lazarus whose new composition was read at the December 3rd opening of the Art Loan Exhibition to benefit the statue of Liberty. (Courtesy, American Jewish Historical Society, Waltham, Mass.)

THE BARTHOLDI STATUE.
Even Liberty demands something substantial to stand upon.

what less than $100,000 had been contributed, including $12,000 from the Art Loan Exhibition. Anywhere between $150,000 and $200,000 remained to be raised.

The press displayed a broad spectrum of opinion regarding the statue. One journal claimed embarrassment that while so many Frenchmen had contributed to the cost of the statue itself, it was the least Americans could do to contribute to funding its base. Another considered France extraordinarily stingy to have presented only the statue, without a foundation on which to mount it. *Harper's Weekly* suggested facetiously that the problems facing both the statue and the still-uncompleted Washington Monument in the capital could easily be resolved by simply affixing Bartholdi's Liberty atop the partially built obelisk.

As of the end of the year, both the New York Academy of Music and the Metropolitan Opera were suffering badly; everyone concluded that the city simply could not support two houses, and that, of course, the Metropolitan should be the one to withdraw. *Bradstreet's*, the financial weekly, reported that the year had witnessed many business failures, more than usual. And on December 31st, Henry Villard resigned from the Northern Pacific Railroad Company.

On the night of December 31st, New Year's Eve, the usual crowd and commotion were awaited at Trinity Church. The activities of both the evening and the following day were expected to be much the same as they had been in past years. There were, however, two important differences. This year, for the first time, Brooklynites would be able to cross the East River to Trinity Church over a bridge. And, unlike all previous years, the year 1884 would be arriving on Standard Time.

Notes

1. Benson J. Lossing, *History of New York City,* vol. 2 (New York: The Perine Engraving and Publishing Co., 1884), p. 812.

2. *Brooklyn Times,* May 5, 1883.

3. *Baldwin's Monthly,* vol. 26, no. 2 (February 1883): 6.

4. *Cigar Makers' Official Journal,* February 1883, p. 6.

5. *The New York Times,* July 20, 1883.

6. *The New York Times,* August 18, 1883.

7. *Brooklyn Daily Eagle,* August 22, 1883.

8. *The New York Times,* February 11, 1883.

9. *The New York Times,* January 8, 1883.

10. *Brooklyn Advance,* vol. 7, no. 2 (April 1883): 85.

11. *The New York Times,* October 27, 1883.

12. *The New York Times,* August 24, 1883.

13. Brooklyn Bureau of Charities, *Second Annual Report,* Brooklyn, 1883, p. 24.

14. *The New York Times,* September 18, 1883.

15. William Graham Sumner, "What Social Classes Owe to Each Other," Part III, *Harper's Weekly,* vol. 27, no. 1368 (March 10, 1883): 157.

16. *Brooklyn Times,* May 5, 1883; May 12, 1883.

17. Henry E. Pierrepont, "Diary," June 25, 1883, The Long Island Historical Society.

18. *New York Tribune,* June 10, 1883.

19. *New York Mirror,* February 17, 1883.

20. *New York Sun,* October 30, 1883.

21. *The New York Times,* January 13, 1883.

22. Manhattan Beach Hotel, *"Carte Du Jour,"* Thursday, July 19, 1883, The Long Island Historical Society.

23. *The New York Times,* May 20, 1883.

24. *The New York Times,* February 4, 1883.

25. *Brooklyn Times,* April 10, 1883.

26. *Brooklyn Times,* April 16, 1883.

27. *New York Herald,* May 15, 1883.

Sources for Quotations in Margin

p. 8. Reverend John Dunlap Wells, "Diary," January 1, 1883, p. 1. The Long Island Historical Society.

p. 17. Appletons' Dictionary of New York and Vicinity (New York: D. Appleton & Co., 1884), p. 44.

p. 23. W.C. Conant, "Will New York Be the Final World Metropolis?", *The Century Magazine*, vol. 26, no. 5 (September 1883): 693.

p. 27. Reginald Fairfax Harrison, "Diary," May 19, 1883, p. 41, Museum of the City of New York.

p. 28. W.C. Conant, "Will New York Be the Final World Metropolis?", p. 693.

p. 29. Harry H. Marks, *Small Change; or, Lights and Shades of New York* (New York: The Standard Publishing Company, 1882), p. 44.

p. 30. Harry H. Marks, *Small Change*, p. 48.

p. 32. Upper: *The New York Times*, July 20, 1883.

p. 32. Lower: *The New York Times*, July 20, 1883.

p. 36. *The New York Times*, July 7, 1883.

p. 37. Mrs. H.M. Plunkett, "The Rosary of Hearts," *Harper's New Monthly Magazine*, vol. 66, no. 392 (January 1883): 236.

p. 39. James C. Bayles, *House Drainage and Water Service*, 3rd edition (New York: David Williams, 1880), p. 97.

p. 41. Upper: Edward Hubbard Litchfield, Letter to Edwin Clark Litchfield, May 1, 1883, Litchfield Papers, Manuscript Division, The New-York Historical Society.

p. 41. Lower: James D. McCabe, *New York by Sunlight and Gaslight* (n.p.: Edgewood Pub. Co., 1882), p. 188.

p. 42. *The New York Times*, April 1, 1883.

p. 43. Upper: *American Architecture and Building News*, vol. 17, no. 373 (February 17, 1883): 77.

p. 43. Lower: Montgomery Schuyler, "Recent Building in New York," *Harper's New Monthly Magazine*, vol. 67, no. 400 (September 1883): 566.

p. 44. "The Problem of Living in New York," *Harper's New Monthly Magazine*, vol. 65, no. 390 (November 1882): 920.

p. 51. Upper: Nathalie Dana, "Lenox Hill in the 1880s. A Girl's Memories of St. James' Parish. Part I: Our House on East 71st Street," *The New-York Historical Society Quarterly*, vol. 46, no. 2 (April 1962): 188.

p. 51. Lower: *Appletons' Dictionary of New York*, p. 56.

p. 54. John Y. Cuyler, "Report of the Chief Engineer and Superintendent," *Report of the Brooklyn Park Commission, January 1, 1884*, in the *Third Annual Message of Hon. Seth Low, Mayor of Brooklyn, Presented to the Honorable Common Council, January 7, 1884*, p. 287.

p. 58. Abraham Cahan, *The Rise of David Levinsky* (New York: Harper & Bros. Publishers, 1917), p. 89.

p. 61. *New York Herald*, February 11, 1883.

p. 63. *The Metropolitan Telephone and Telegraph Company Subscribers' List*, February 15, 1883, p. 2.

p. 64. *The New York Times*, August 26, 1883.

p. 66. *The New York Times*, January 6, 1883.

p. 67. *The New York Times,* editorial, October 15, 1883.

p. 72. Upper: *The New York Times,* August 13, 1883.

p. 72. Lower: "Charity Organization," *Harper's Weekly,* vol. 27, no. 1409 (December 22, 1883): 811.

p. 74. *The New York Times,* editorial, August 24, 1883.

p. 79. George Cary Eggleston, "The Education of Women," *Harper's New Monthly Magazine,* vol. 67, no. 348 (July 1883): 295.

p. 80. *White, Stokes, & Allen's Guide and Select Directory. What to See and Where to Buy in New York City* (New York: White, Stokes, & Allen, 1884), p. 127.

p. 82. *New York World,* May 11, 1883.

p. 83. Upper: *The New York Times,* July 7, 1883; *New York Herald,* March 8, 1883.

p. 83. Middle: Reginald Fairfax Harrison, "Diary," May 7, 1883, p 18.

p. 83. Lower: *The New York Times,* October 28, 1883.

p. 86. Upper: *New York Sun,* April 29, 1883.

p. 86. Lower: Charles H. Crandall, ed., *The Season, An Annual Record of Society in New York, Brooklyn, and Vicinity* (New York: White, Stokes, & Allen, 1883), p. 10.

p. 88. *Brooklyn Advance,* vol. 7, no. 1 (March 1883): 52.

p. 89. Upper: Jenny June, "How We Live in New York. Transformation Scenes and Seasons," *Demorest's Monthly Magazine,* vol. 20, no. 2 (December 1883): 100.

p. 89. Lower: Edith Wharton, *The Age of Innocence* (New York: D. Appleton and Company, 1920), p. 258.

p. 91. James William Buel, *The Mysteries and Miseries of America's Great Cities* (San Francisco: A.L. Bancroft & Co., 1883), p. 52.

p. 92. M.G. van Rensselaer, "Spring Exhibitions in New York—III," *American Architecture and Building News,* vol. 13, no. 387 (May 26, 1883): 244.

p. 93. *New York Herald,* March 15, 1883.

p. 94. *New York Evening Post,* April 24, 1883.

p. 101. Reginald Fairfax Harrison, "Diary," May 12, 1883, p. 27.

p. 104. Upper: Henry E. Pierrepont, "Diary," March 19, 1883, The Long Island Historical Society.

p. 104. Lower: Reginald Fairfax Harrison, "Diary," May 12, 1883, p. 27.

p. 105. Reginald Fairfax Harrison, "Diary," May 24, 1883, pp. 52-56.

p. 109. *New York Daily Tribune,* October 23, 1883.

p. 111. *The New York Times,* November 27, 1883.

Bibliographical Note

An enormous array of primary source material was used in order to recreate aspects of the two cities in the year 1883. For the most part, secondary sources were limited to those published in the early 1880s. The two major contemporary sources are Benson J. Lossing, *History of New York City,* 1884, and Henry R. Stiles, compiler of *The Civil, Political, Professional and Ecclesiastical History and Commercial and Industrial Record of the County of Kings and the City of Brooklyn,* 1884. Twentieth-century sources in such areas as social, labor, political history, and biography were used only as points of reference, and even the remarkable I.N. Phelps Stokes *Iconography of Manhattan Island* was of limited value for this study.

Official documents included U.S. Census reports, legislative records and statutes, court proceedings and reports, and municipal and county reports and records as well as mayoral papers. The many daily and weekly newspapers, and monthly magazines were a particularly rich and important source of information. Guidebooks and city directories were also valuable resources. The annual reports and archives of organizations and institutions constituted yet another useful source. Diaries, letters, and scrapbooks located at the Library of Congress, the Long Island Historical Society, the Museum of the City of New York, the New-York Historical Society, and the New York Public Library offered added dimension to the more formal resources. And novels and short stories of the period provided additional insights.

Photograph, print, map, and picture collections furnished valuable information. Material drawn upon included photographs, prints, drawings, portraits, playbills, advertisements, and a broad assortment of ephemera such as trade cards, invitations, tickets, and programs. A variety of maps—including atlases, insurance maps, guidebook maps, and ward maps—provided essential data.